The Mental Health Act Commission

Sixth Biennial Report 1993–1995

Laid before Parliament by the Secretary of State for Health pursuant to Section 121 (10) of the Mental Health Act 1983

London: HMSO

Table of Contents

Section III

Section IV   Priorities in Community Care

Section V

Section VI   Appendices

Chairman's Foreword

In his foreword to the last Biennial Report, my predecessor, Sir Louis Blom-Cooper QC, described the Mental Health Act Commission entering upon a process of self-examination and change. Two years later, and coincident with the publication of its sixth Report, the restructured and enlarged Commission is equipped to pursue its statutory duties with a greatly enhanced visiting capacity, and new scope to target its activities.

The elements of the change are described elsewhere in this report. What is not described is how much the process has demanded of the administrative staff and members of the Commission alike. It has involved the Commission in revising its structure, examining and refining all its policies and procedures, developing its specialist capacities and mounting a national recruitment exercise at the same time as continuing to fulfil the functions for which it exists. Self-scrutiny is a healthy exercise for a watchdog body more used to scrutinising others, and I would like to pay tribute to the open-mindedness and vigour with which the task has been tackled by all those involved.

The task of the next two years is to ensure that these changes are subjected to rigorous quality control, and that the Commission develops its ability to use effectively the much greater flow of information which the changes will generate, in the interests of patients, practitioners and policy makers.

There remains an important gap in the Commission's ability to do its work. Since its inception, it has pointed to the desirability for it to be informed of every detention and discharge as is the case with its sister bodies in Scotland and Northern Ireland. That gap is all the more glaring when the latest Mental Health Act statistics (for 1991-3) from the Department of Health show a steadily increasing use of the Mental Health Act, with no concomitant understanding of the reasons for this increased use. It is salutary to realise that in 1774, in the very first Act for regulation of houses where mentally ill people were confined, notice of all new patients had to be sent within three days to the Secretary of the Commission.

The past two years have been a challenging time for all involved in mental health services. The Fifth Biennial Report highlighted the intense pressure on acute psychiatric services in the inner cities. The Commission has seen no significant improvement in this situation; moreover, it has found that these problems are no longer confined to metropolitan areas, and appear to be accompanied also by a marked increase in disturbed behaviour amongst patients admitted to these services. Whilst there is little disagreement among professionals about the unwanted effects of these trends or about the remedies, what remains is the gap between what is needed and the consistent ability of services to respond.

Among the Secretary of State's responses to the acknowledged difficulties of ensuring aftercare has been the Mental Health (Patients in the Community) Bill. The Commission is disappointed that an important encroachment on individual liberty has not been accompanied by an equivalent protection of the individual's rights and interests. We particularly regret that advantage was not taken of the Commission's increased capacity to handle an extension of its remit at low cost. It is clear that the fundamental review of the Mental Health Act about which there is widespread agreement is some way off. Meanwhile, there are some important intermediate improvements required which are the victims of a climate of postponement. The Commission believes that extending its remit to cover patients under guardianship, as recommended by the Law Commission, and patients subject to aftercare under supervision are two such necessary changes.

The period since the publication of the Commission's last Biennial Report has also been punctuated by the findings of a series of enquiries - Clunis, Buchanan, Robinson, Laudat among them - all of which have exposed the fault-lines in the co-ordination of care. They have, inevitably, contributed to public doubts about the ability of Community Care to ensure the safety of patients or the public. The danger is that these doubts become translated into fear of serious mental illness and those who suffer from it, and into a belief that the institutional response is the only acceptable one, a view as misplaced as that which holds that such a response is never justified. We must prevent this polarisation of views if the advances of the last twenty years are to be preserved and built upon. A process of public education is needed. Crucial to this process is the informed contribution of the media, in particular the press, as well as the willingness of all those involved in mental health services - including the Commission - to play their part.

Ruth Runciman

Rhagair Y Cadeirydd

Yn ei ragair i'r Adroddiad Eilflwyddol diwethaf disgrifiodd fy rhagflaenydd, Syr Louis Blom-Cooper QC, sut roedd Comisiwn y Ddeddf Iechyd Meddwl yn cychwyn ar broses o hunan-archwilio ac o newid. Ddwy flynedd yn ddiweddarach, ac yn cyd-daro â chyhoeddi'i chweched Adroddiad, mae'r Comisiwn, ar ôl iddo gael ei ail-strwythuro a'i ehangu, yn barod i ddilyn ei ddyletswyddau statudol gyda gallu llawer iawn helaethach yng nhyd-destun ymweld, a chwmpas newydd i dargedu ei weithgareddau.

Disgrifir elfennaur newid mewn mannau eraill yn yr adroddiad. Yr hyn nas disgrifir yw'r pwysau a olygodd y newid i'r staff gweinyddol ac i aelodau'r Comisiwn, y naill fel y llall. Bu'n rhaid i'r Comisiwn adolygu ei strwythur, archwilio a rhoi min ar ei holl bolisïau a'i drefniadaeth, datblygu ei fedrau arbenigol a threfnu ymgyrch recriwtio cenedlaethol yngyd â pharhau i gyflawni'i swyddogaethau sylfaenol. Mae hunan-archwiliad yn ymarfer buddiol ar gyfer mudiad gwarchodol sy'n fwy cyfarwydd ag archwilio gwaith eraill. Hoffwn dalu teyrnged i'r ffordd ystyriol a grymus y mae pawb wedi ymgodymu â'r dasg.

Y dasg ar gyfer y ddwy flynedd nesaf yw sicrhau rheolaeth ansawdd lem ar gyfer y newidiadau hyn. Hefyd, rhaid i'r Comisiwn ddatblygu'i allu i wneud defnydd effeithiol o'r llif mwy sylweddol o wybodaeth a grëir gan y newidiadau, er budd cleifion, ymarferwyr a llunwyr polisi.

Mae bwlch pwysig yn parhau yng ngallu'r Comisiwn i wneud ei waith. O'r cychwyn cyntaf, soniwyd am yr angen am fanylion am bob un sy'n cael ei gadw o dan y Ddeddf Iechyd Meddwl ac sy'n cael ei ryddhau, fel sy'n digwydd gyda'i chwaer gyrff yn yr Alban ac yng Ngogledd Iwerddon. Mae'r bwlch yn fwy dybrid fyth pan yw'r ystadegau diweddaraf ynglŷn â'r Ddeddf Iechyd Meddwl (ar gyfer 1991-3) a ddaw o'r Adran Iechyd yn dangos defnydd cynyddol o'r Ddeddf, heb fod unrhyw ddealltwriaeth gyfatebol o'r rhesymau dros y defnydd cynyddol hwn. Mae'n drawiadol sylweddoli fod y ddeddf gyntaf, ym 1774, i reoli'r tai lle cedwid pobl ... d meddwl yn mynnu fod rhaid danfon manylion ar gyfer bob claf newydd i ... fennydd y Comisiwn o fewn tridiau.

Bu'r ddwy flynedd diwethaf yn gyfnod o sialenns ar gyfer pawb sy'n ymwneud âr gwasanaethau iechyd meddwl. Yn y Pumed Adroddiad Eilflwyddol pwysleisiwyd y ffaith fod y gwasanaethau seiciatregol llym yng nghanol y dinasoed o dan bwysau aruthrol. Ni welodd y Comisiwn unrhyw welliant arwyddocaol yn y sefyllfa. Yn wir, cafwyd nad yw'r problemau hyn mwyach yn gyfyngedig i'r ardaloedd dinesig. Yn cydredeg â hyn gwelwyd cynnydd mewn ymddygiad ymosodol ymhlith y cleifion a dderbynir gan y gwasanaethau hyn. Nid oes fawr ddim anghytundeb ymhlith gweithwyr proffesiynol ynglŷn ag effeithiau annymunol y tueddiadau hyn nac am y meddyginiaethau. Yr hyn sydd yn aros yw'r gagendor rhwng yr hyn sydd ei angen a gallu'r gwasanaethau i ymateb â chysondeb i'r galw.

Ymhlith ymatebion yr Ysgrifennydd Gwladol i'r anawsterau cydnabyddedig o sicrhau ôl-ofal yw'r Mesur Iechyd Meddwl (Cleifion yn y Gymuned). Ceir cyfyngiad pwysig ar ryddid yr unigolyn ac mae'r Comisiwn yn siomedig nad oes ymgais cyfatebol i warchod hawliau a buddiannau'r unigolyn. Rydym yn gresynu'n benodol na chymerwyd mantais ar alluoedd ehangach y Comisiwn i fod yn gyfrifol am y dyletswyddau ychwanegol hyn er mai bychan fyddai'r gost. Mae'n amlwg fod yr adolygiad sylfaenol o'r Ddeddf Iechyd Meddwl, y mae cymaint cytundeb yn ei gylch, yn dal yn bell i ffwrdd. Yn y cyfamser mae'r duedd hon i ohirio yn rhwystro nifer o welliannau canolradd psysig. Cred y Comisiwn fod estyn ei gyfrifoldebau i gynnwys cleifion o dan warcheidwaeth, fel yr argymhellwyd gan Gomisiwn y Gyfraith, a chleifion sy'n cael ôl-ofal o dan oruchwyliaeth, yn ddau newid angenrheidiol.

Yn y cyfnod oddi ar cyhoeddi Adroddiad Eilflwyddol ola'r Comisiwn cafwyd canlyniadau cyfres o ymholiadau - Clunis, Buchanan, Torbay, Rous yn eu plith - maent i gyd wedi dinoethi'r ffawtlinau yng nghyd-drefniant gofal. Yn anochel, maent wedi cyfrannu at amheuon y cyhoedd ynglŷn â gallu gofal yn y gymuned i sicrhau diogelwch y cleifion a'r cyhoedd fel y'i gilydd. Y perygl yw y bydd yr amheuon hyn yn troi'n ofn ynglŷn ag afeichyd meddwl difrifol ac yn ofn o'r rhai sy'n dioddef ohono ac y bydd y gred yn datblygu mai ymateb sefydliadol yw'r unig un derbyniol. Mae afbwynt o'r fath yr un mor anghywir â'r un sy'n mynnu nad oes byth gyfiawnhad i'r math yma a ymateb. Rhaid i ni rwystro'r polareiddiad hwn mewn safbwyntiau os ydym am ddiogelu ac adeiladu ar welliannau'r ugain mlynedd diwethaf. Mae angen proses o addysgu'r cyhoedd. Elfen angenrheidiol o'r broses hon yw cyfraniad deallus y cyfryngau, yn enwedig y wasg, yngyd â pharodrwydd ar ran pawb sydd ynglân â'r gwasanaethau iechyd meddwl - gan gynnwys y Comisiwn - i chwarae'u rhan.

Ruth Runciman

Section I

The Commission

1   *The Evolving Structure of the Commission*

1.1   The New Organisation of the Mental Health Act Commission

The Mental Health Act Commission is a Special Health Authority which, on behalf of the Secretary of State, keeps under review the use of the Mental Health Act in England and Wales in relation to patients detained in hospital under the Act.

Further details about the Commission's role and function are outlined in Appendix 1.

Members of the Commission have continued to visit the Special Hospitals, Regional and other secure units, general psychiatric facilities and Registered Mental Nursing Homes. Each member is allocated to one of seven visiting teams (CVTs) serving areas coterminous with Regional Health Authorities and also to one of three Special Hospital Panels (SHPs).

Following the centralisation of the Commission's administrative offices in 1990, a process of refining Commission policies and administrative procedures was embarked upon. In the last Biennial Report the Commission recorded that it had been successful in achieving the objectives of centralisation, but noted that the process of reviewing Commission procedures should remain an on-going concern. Particular attention has been paid since that time to the administration of its complaints jurisdiction, the consent to treatment arrangements and the evolution of agreed policies.

However, the Commission is aware of areas of its work where Commission activity can still be improved. For example, the current procedure of visiting most psychiatric hospitals only once every year has meant that only a small proportion of detained patients are seen by Commission members. The Commission is also concerned to strengthen its centre to enable it to adapt to the significant changes in the delivery of mental health care. The restructuring of the Commission, first proposed in the Fifth Biennial Report (Chapter 16), aims to meet these challenges.

The proposal to restructure the Commission fundamentally, within the constraints of a fixed budget, was agreed by the Minister in November 1994.

This process, which had to be achieved within the current resource allocation, will be largely completed by 1st November 1995.

Objectives of the Changes

- *To increase the quality and quantity of contact time between members of the Mental Health Act Commission and patients.*

  It is hoped this will be achieved by the introduction of "visiting members" of the Commission whose primary, but not exclusive, role will be to visit detained patients in hospital. Most units will receive "patient only" visits two or three times a year. It is hoped that the appointment of visiting members, who will be based more locally to the places which they visit, will make it easier for the Commission to relate more effectively to the growing number of locality based services. Other Commission visits will include detailed discussions with senior management and other interested parties and will be more targeted. The Commission's practice of visiting each unit in this way once a year has been changed to take into account the need to concentrate resources on areas of particular interest or concern.

  All units will initially receive such a visit at least once every two years.

- *To improve the way in which the Commission undertakes its complaints remit.*

  A member of the Commission has been appointed as "Complaints Co-ordinator". He will be based in the Commission's Nottingham office 3 days per week and will take responsibility for overseeing the Commission's complaints remit.

- *To improve the Commission's data collection system and the recording and feedback of information.*

  Improving information systems will enhance the Commission's monitoring capacity and the systematic collection of data will better serve the needs of independent researchers. In the future, such improvement would be enhanced if the Commission was notified of all detentions and discharges under the 1983 Act.

1.2   Changes In The Commission Structure

The Commission has introduced a more defined management hierarchy for its members. Individual duties are now more sharply defined and there will be different scales of remuneration to reflect the responsibilities of individual members of the Commission.

- *"Area Managers" have been appointed to manage each of the geographically based Commission Visiting Teams and three Special Hospitals Panels.*

- *A Policy Commission member will be based in the administration office three days a week, who will strengthen the Commission's ability to respond quickly and effectively to policy matters, together with the development of a Standing Policy Committee.*

- *The Central Policy Committee will be replaced by a Management Board of a similar composition to that found in other Health Authorities and by a new small Policy Committee.*

The new structure is to be supported by a more open recruitment, enhanced training and annual appraisal of Commission members.

The recruitment exercise, held in May 1995, yielded a large number of applications enabling Ministers to make appointments from a group of potential members representing a promising distribution of professions, age groups, gender, ethnic background and skills.

For the first time since the Commission's inception, an open recruitment process has been introduced. It was decided to invite applications for membership of the Commission as part of the restructuring process. An advertisement was placed in one national broadsheet newspaper and five professional magazines. Within 24 hours of the advertisement appearing, over 100 enquiries had been received in the office and more than 700 applications were received within the 14 day deadline. A separate and anonymous ethnic monitoring form was sent with each set of application forms and 74% of them were returned. The number of applications was reduced to manageable proportions by taking into account the geographical distribution of vacancies and the multi-disciplinary composition of the visiting teams. This resulted in 248 candidates being short-listed for 138 vacancies. A total of 30 interview panels were held throughout England and Wales and a total of 27 new members and 115 visiting members were appointed.

Of the 74% of applicants who returned the forms, 15% were from ethnic minorities. Of the 248 interviewed, 13% were from ethnic minorities as were 13% of those appointed.

It is anticipated that the combination of these reforms and innovations will enhance the overall effectiveness of the Commission and individual Commission members.

The strengthening of the centre should improve the speed with which the Commission can comment on general issues arising out of the operation of the Act. Information on different units will be improved through more frequent and targeted visiting.

1.3   The Development of a Commission "Special Procedure" in Relation to Bad Practice

The Commission has long been concerned about its lack of statutory sanctions in relation to persistent bad practice, since it possesses only three "executive" powers, which are to:

- visit and interview in private, patients detained under the Mental Health Act

- require the production of and inspect any records relating to the detention or treatment of any person who is, or who has been, detained in a Registered Mental Nursing Home (Section 121(4), see footnote 1) or hospital (DHSS Circular No HC 83/19)

- overrule decisions by the managers of Special Hospitals to withhold patients' mail (Section 134)

The Commission is currently seeking the approval of the Department of Health to implement a special administrative procedure where a matter of persistent and serious concern that falls within the Commission's statutory remit is noted during a Commission visit to a hospital or arises in the course of investigating a complaint.

The special procedure will be used sparingly, with prior authority from the Chairman of the Commission and only where there are persistent serious breaches of the Mental Health Act or Code of Practice.

Information about the use of the procedure, if it is adopted, will be included in future Biennial Reports.

---

[1] In this Report, all references to Sections or Sections of the Act refer to Sections of the Mental Health Act (1983)

1.4   The Commission's Future Remit

The Commission's remit is confined currently to patients detained under the Mental Health Act. There has been a standing request with Ministers since 1985 that the remit of the Commission should be extended to "de facto" detained patients.

In its Fifth Biennial Report, the Commission said:

> *"The Commission considers that there are groups of people receiving care and treatment for mental disorder in a variety of situations who are subject to elements of compulsion or substitute decision-making and whose rights are not effectively protected".*

That position has not changed over the last two years.

The Mental Health (Patients in the Community) Bill, published in 1993, aims to provide a new legal framework for the supervision of some detained patients who have been discharged from hospital.

The Bill includes new powers of control which can be imposed on patients under Supervised Discharge. The Commission suggested in its public position paper that the proposed introduction of these additional powers warranted consideration being given to the extension of its remit to such patients to enable it to ensure as far as possible that:

- the new powers are correctly exercised and applied in strict accordance with the statutory guidelines, and

- by monitoring the new provision over a number of years to recommend whether the use of these powers is of benefit to the patients involved and the community to which they have been discharged.

At the time of going to press, the Bill had completed Committee stage in the House of Commons.

The extension of the Commission's remit to those under guardianship was recommended by the Law Commission (paragraph 9.52 of the Law Commission Report No: 231 on Mental Incapacity dated 28th February 1995)

Section II

General Issues

2   *Legal Issues and Enquiries*

Introduction

During the last two years there have been a number of legal cases relating to the interpretation and application of the Mental Health Act 1983. It is certain that the Act will continue to pose problems of construction and interpretation for discussion, comment and occasionally for resolution by courts.

In recognition of the fact that the Commission has within its membership a unique combination of talents from medical, social, nursing, legal, administrative and other specialist members, it has been decided to set up a sub-group to identify and consider legal issues. It is hoped that the group will address the issues raised in a practical and pragmatic manner while recognising the importance of the words of the Act and the intentions behind the rules and regulations which regulate the care and treatment of patients who are detained or are liable to be detained in hospital under the Mental Health Act 1983.

In its Fifth Biennial Report, the Mental Health Act Commission suggested that the Mental Health Act 1983 be subject to a full review with the aim of proposing new legislation to reflect changes in the provision of psychiatric treatment and care for people suffering from mental disorder. This remains the Commission's considered opinion. However, there has been no such review and the provisions of the Mental Health Act 1983 continue to attract the interest of the courts. There has also been a major review by the Law Commission of decision-making on personal matters, including consent to medical treatment.

2.1   Cases Relating to Definition of Medical Treatment and Psychopathic Disorder

Reference was made in paragraph 12.7 of the Fifth Biennial Report to the case of R -v- Canons Park Mental Health Review Tribunal, ex parte A. The Court of Appeal in 1994 (reported at (1994) 3 WLR 630) reversed an earlier decision and provided useful guidance on the treatability test. The court considered this both in the context of a discharge by a Mental Health Review Tribunal and in the wider area of admission criteria for patients who are described as psychopaths. The interpretation of the phrase "medical treatment" and the "treatability test" has been a matter of concern for some time. A Department of Health/Home Office Working Group was established in 1992 to review the treatment of people with personality and psychopathic disorder, their appropriate location and the arrangements for placing offenders in need of treatment and/or detention in prison. It reported in 1994[1]. The working group also considered whether the definition of mental disorder or psychopathic disorder should be included in the Mental Health Act. This has been a matter of controversy since the implementation of the Mental Health Act 1959.

In the above case, the three members of the Court of Appeal divided two to one but it was decided, by a majority decision, that when considering "treatability" under the Mental Health Act, regard must be had to the broad statutory definition of treatment. This is defined at Section 145 of the Mental Health Act as "nursing, and also includes care, habilation and rehabilitation under medical supervision". The court further decided that a patient's refusal to co-operate in such treatment does not necessarily render that patient untreatable. The test to be applied, either at admission or at discharge of a patient with psychopathic disorder or mental impairment, is whether or not treatment was likely to alleviate or prevent a deterioration in the patient's condition. This is set out in the Mental Health Act at Section 3(1)(b).

The division in the Court of Appeal and the strong contrary judgements in the Divisional Court indicate that this is an area which may be reviewed by the courts during the next few years.

In B -v- the Croydon Health Authority (1995) 2 WLR 294, the Court of Appeal considered the definition of "Medical Treatment" within the terms of Section 63 of the 1983 Act. The court also considered the question of consent to treatment generally. In this case the patient was diagnosed as suffering from a psychopathic disorder described as "a borderline personality disorder". The disorder included depression and a compulsion to self harm, including self starvation. During her admission to hospital under Section 3 the patient virtually stopped eating. The patient was threatened with feeding by naso-gastric tube and applied to the High Court for an injunction to prevent this happening. The High Court held that tube feeding would be lawful and would be included in the definition "medical treatment for a mental disorder". Section 63 of the Mental Health Act 1983 provides that medical treatment for a mental disorder, not being treatment falling within Section 57 or 58, may be given without consent of the patient and the court considered that tube feeding was treatment within this definition.

The Court of Appeal upheld this decision.

In his judgement, Lord Justice Hoffman said:-

> *"The general law is that an adult person of full mental capacity has the right to choose whether to eat or not. Even if the refusal to eat is tantamount to suicide, as in the case of a hunger strike, he cannot be compelled to eat or be forcibly fed. On the other hand, if a person lacks the mental capacity to choose, by the common law the medical practitioner who has him in his care may treat him (and by this I include the artificial administration of food) according to his clinical judgement of the patient's best interest. In addition, under Section 63 of the Mental Health Act 1983, the consent of a patient liable to be detained under the Act is not required for "any treatment given to him for the mental disorder from which he is suffering ....".*

> *Lord Justice Neil also said "I am satisfied that the words in Section 63 of the Mental Health Act 1983, '...any medical treatment given to him for the mental disorder from which he is suffering...', include "treatment given to him to alleviate the symptoms of the disorder as well as treatment to remedy its underlying cause". In the first place it seems to me that it would often be difficult in practice for those treating a patient to draw a clear distinction between procedures or parts of procedures which were designed to treat the disorder itself and those procedures or parts which were designed to treat its symptoms and sequelae. In my view the medical treatment has to be looked at as a whole and this approach is reinforced by the wide definition of "medical treatment" in Section 145(1) as including "nursing" and also "care habilitation and rehabilitation under medical supervision"."*

This case followed a number of similar cases, including Re C (Adult .... refusal of treatment) (1994) 1 WLR 290, Riverside Mental Health NHS Trust -v- Fox (1) (1994) 1 FLR 614 and Re T (Adult .... refusal of treatment) (1993) Family 1995, all of which considered the question of capacity of an individual to consent to his or her own treatment and the responsibilities of the health care system to provide treatment with or without the patient's consent.

2.2 Cases Concerned With Admission Criteria

The Commission is anxious to ensure that the admission criteria set out in the 1983 Mental Health Act are correctly applied and that the correct section is used to authorise the patient's detention. It is also important that the appropriate forms are correctly completed and that admission procedures are followed. The Mental Health Act Commission welcomes the decision in R -v- Ex parte Williamson (1995) A 11ER. In this case the High Court held that admission for an assessment under Section 2 of the Mental Health Act 1983 could not be extended beyond twenty-eight days, except where Section 29 (4) applies, i.e. when an application is made by the Social Services Authority to displace a nearest relative who objects to the implementation of a Section 3. The court further decided that Section 2 could never be used where the purpose of the admission was not for assessment (or assessment followed by treatment) but was for detention in hospital for treatment.

Mr Justice Tucker said in this case *"in my opinion the scheme contemplated by the legislation is clear. An order made under Section 2 is only intended to be of short duration for a limited purpose/assessment of the patient's condition with a view to ascertaining whether it is a case which would respond to treatment, and whether an order under Section 3 would be appropriate".* The Mental Health Act Code of Practice (Chapter 5) gives guidance on the distinction between the implementation of Section 2 and Section 3.

The criteria for the admission of a patient to hospital was commented upon in "The Falling Shadow" (a report published in 1995 on the care and treatment of Andrew Robinson who was convicted of the murder in 1993 of Georgina Robinson). This report addresses many issues, including "the deteriorating patient" and concluded that where a patient or ex-patient in the community ceased to take medication and was without symptoms, compulsory admission may be appropriate in certain circumstances "without waiting for the psychosis to ripen". This would be an informed clinical decision based upon the patient's present clinical state, his or her history and in particular whether or not cessation of medication has led in the past to a deterioration of the patient's condition.

This inquiry also considered the use of leave of absence under Section 17 of the Mental Health Act 1983. The Commission is concerned that the implementation of Section 17 is not always carefully monitored or carried out in accordance with the provisions of the Act on the Code of Practice.

2.3 Mental Incapacity

The common law requires that a medical practitioner must comply with clear instructions given by an adult of sound mind as to the treatment to be given or not given in certain circumstances, whether those instructions are rational or irrational[2]. Part IV of the Mental Health Act 1983 overrides these considerations for patients who are detained under the Act for treatment of their mental disorder.

Valid consent is dependent on the capacity to make decisions. The Law Commission has now produced its final report[3],[4] making wide recommendations for reform in the complex area of decision-making by mentally incapacitated adults. The Mental Health Act Commission has responded to the various interim papers produced by the Law Commission.

The Mental Health Act Commission welcomes the report, especially in relation to those with learning disability and some of the elderly mentally ill. Proposals include changes in emergency powers of intervention (paragraphs 9.19 - 9.28), statutory Second Opinions in relation to treatment of incapacitated patients, including those not formally detained (paragraphs 6.11 - 6.15), and changes to the way in which an incapacitated patient may enter into formal detention (paragraphs 8.27 - 8.29).

The Law Commission recommends that the powers of a Guardian under Section 7 of the Mental Health Act 1983 should be extended to include a power to convey, and that the remit of the Mental Health Act Commission be extended to cover Guardianship. The report also includes proposals for a new Court of Protection and for a new Continuing Power of Attorney with enhanced powers to replace the existing Enduring Power of Attorney. The new power would include within its domain health care, consent to treatment and, possibly, the concept of advance refusal of treatment, which could be of significance in relation to Part IV of the Mental Health Act. The report also proposes the development of a new Code of Practice to accompany any legislation.

3   *Code of Practice*

The revised Code of Practice was published in August 1993[5] and there is a growing awareness of its existence and importance to providing high standards of care within the framework of the Mental Health Act. Increasingly, hospitals are including it in formal training programmes and this is a welcome development. However, Commission members still find that some staff are inexcusably unaware of the Code.

The Commission is pursuing another way to ensure that the Code is more adequately implemented. It is encouraging the development of quality standards based on the Code which purchasing authorities can incorporate into their contracts and service agreements with provider units. This guidance for health commissions (purchasers) is in preparation.

Particular issues that are regularly seen as problematical by Commission members on their visits to hospitals include scrutiny of documents, use of doctors' holding powers under Section 5(2), good practice in documenting the presentation and understanding by patients of their rights under the Mental Health Act (Section 132), consent to treatment and good practice in completing consent forms and documenting attempts to obtain valid consent, the granting of Section 17 leave, the documenting and provision of adequate after-care under Section 117 and the inclusion of all relevant personnel, including involved families and carers in devising the care plans[6]. These issues are discussed in detail below.

Some of the new developments in the provision of health care, such as the formation of NHS Trusts and the burgeoning provision of mental health care, especially medium secure provisions by private Registered Mental Nursing Homes, were not anticipated at the time when the Mental Health Act was introduced and some provisions of the Act and the Code of Practice do not adequately address these changes. Some of the issues are highlighted below, together with other areas in which the Commission feels that some revision of the Code of Practice is warranted. Many of these issues will recur in different places in this report.

As an example of the extent of deviation from the Code of Practice, a number of errors found by members of the Commission in just one visit are highlighted below.

> *At Sutton Manor Hospital on a single visit, inspection of the statutory documents revealed the following errors.*
>
> *Section 1 - Definition of Mental Disorder: patient admitted because of alcohol abuse*
>
> *Section 4 - Emergency Application for Admission: admission not effected within 24 hours*
>
> *Section 5(2) - Reasons given did not indicate why an application should be made*
>
> *Section 11, 26- Nearest relative application: misunderstanding of definition of the nearest relative. Application made by the wrong person*
>
> *Section 12(3),(4),(5) (d) and (e): medical recommendations unacceptable. They were made by a doctor with a financial interest, plus a practitioner on the staff of the hospital*
>
> *Section 12- Joint medical recommendation form used when examination did not take place on the same day (Code of Practice 2.23). Second doctor made no entries of his own, mainly just countersigning the statements of the first doctor. Members of the Commission felt that the joint medical recommendation for a Section 3 was inadequate*
>
> *Sections 20, 23, Reviews of liability to detention: reviews were not carried out regularly*
>
> *Section 17 Leave of absence: no authorisation by the RMO*
>
> *Section 23-25, Discharge by nearest relative: nearest relative's intention to discharge was not notified to the RMO before the discharge took place*

3.1 Admission to Hospital (Section 2, 3 and 4)

There is some concern over the 'misuse' of Section 2 where Section 3 would be more appropriate in cases of patients well known to the service with long established mental health problems (see also Chapter 2.2).

The use of Section 4 appears to be high in some areas where there is a lack of availability of Section 12 approved doctors. In other areas where they are readily available (which are the majority) its use is extremely low. There has been an improvement in the use of audit on this Section, and when audit systems have been introduced, assessments for Section 2 or 3 have been implemented earlier.

> ***Burnley Healthcare NHS Trust*** *– use of Section*
>
> *Members of the Commission have raised with the managers of Burnley Healthcare NHS Trust their concern over the high ratio (3 to 1) of Section 2 usage compared to Section 3. They have also noted the repeated use of Section 2 within relatively short intervening periods. The Commission emphasised the guidance in the Code of Practice (Chapter 5) and the recommendation that patients who are well known to the service and who have long histories of mental illness are ordinarily more suitably placed under Section 3 than Section 2. The use of Section 2 disadvantages patients as they lose their statutory rights to Section 117 aftercare, which is an important aspect of care under Section 3. The Commission found on its most recent visit that there had been a marked improvement in the situation and that Section 3 was being used for patients previously known to the services.*

3.2 Scrutiny of Documents / Medical Records / Flagging Systems

The growing number of Mental Health Act Administrators of high calibre in mental health units has led to an overall improvement in the standards of preparation and scrutiny of documents relating to the detention and care of patients detained under the Act, although medical scrutiny of medical recommendations does not always take place.

There is some good practice developing with respect to communication between Trusts and GPs, regarding GP medical recommendations.

> ***Royal Oldham Hospital - Medical Scrutiny of Section Papers***
>
> *The Clinical Director has devised a feedback form which is used in all instances. Members of the Commission commend this approach as a way of increasing knowledge and understanding of the Mental Health Act and also of providing positive reinforcement of good practice.*

3.3 Second Medical Recommendation.

The Act requires that one (but not more than one) of the medical practitioners shall be on the staff of the hospital to which it is proposed to admit a patient, except under certain clearly defined conditions (Section 12(3)). There has been some concern that this would preclude the second medical recommendation from being provided by a doctor on the staff of another hospital but employed by the same Trust as the first. It is the Commission view that this is not the case.

3.4 The Relative / Nearest Relative Under the Act (Sections 11, 13, 26)

Members of the Commission are sometimes asked for guidance about the definition of the Nearest Relative under the Act. This can be found at Section 26 of the Act which sets out the rules for determining the Nearest Relative, who is frequently not the person regarded as next of kin, in each case.

Although attention is usually paid by Approved Social Workers (ASWs) to the requirement under Section 11 of the Act to inform or consult the Nearest Relative about an admission under a Section of the Act and of the power to discharge from detention under Section 23, there remain occasions when this requirement is overlooked. Similarly, there is a requirement under Section 13(1) of the Act for the ASW to *"have regard to the wishes expressed by relatives of the patient"* in relation to an admission and, under Section 13(4), *"to inform the Nearest Relative of his reasons in writing if in any case the social worker decides not to make an application"* in those cases where the Nearest Relative has exercised his/her power under that subsection: these requirements are not always implemented.

Some Departmental guidelines[6] have also referred to families and involved carers, particularly in relation to the implementation of care packages on discharge from hospital, and these concepts could usefully be incorporated into a revised Code of Practice.

3.5 Doctors' Holding Powers Under Section 5(2).

Although practice is improving, the Commission still finds that an unacceptably high proportion of detentions under Section 5(2) lapse without further assessment being made after the full course of 72 hours, or run for periods in excess of 60 hours before assessment for a Section 2 or 3 under the Act is undertaken. In some areas the high use of Section 5(2) shortly after admission indicates the absence of proper assessment taking place prior to patients' admission. There are still hospitals where staff believe that Part IV of the Act applies to Section 5(2) patients.

There has, however, been a welcome increase in the use of audit on this section and, where this has occurred, it has generally resulted in early assessment and much improved practice. Audit of the use of the Section has sometimes, but not invariably, shown that there is a high use of the Section at weekends or at times which could be considered as 'unsocial'. This indicates that the section is not being employed as recommended in the Code of Practice (8.1-16).

The Code of Practice (8.13-8.16) gives guidance on the nomination of a deputy to exercise Section 5(2) powers in the absence of the Registered Medical Practitioner (RMP). The nominated deputy may often be the junior doctor on call but it is the duty of the RMP to ensure that he has nominated a deputy for every duty period (the term Responsible Medical Officer (RMO) is defined in Section 34 of the Act). [7],[8]

Stockport Healthcare NHS Trust – use of sections 5(2) & 5(4)

The use of these holding powers at Stepping Hill and St Thomas' Hospitals demonstrates the most striking evidence of the good practice that members of the Commission have noted during their visits there. Those patients held on Section 5(2) were all seen by a consultant within 24 hours and there were no instances of the Section being used to hold patients over a weekend. A checklist provided for the guidance of junior staff by the Trust seems to have been most effective. There has been only a necessity to have recourse to Section 5(4) on four occasions over the last year and these patients were seen by a doctor after a minimal delay.

3.6   Leave under Section 17

The implementation of Section 17 of the Mental Health Act is a matter of considerable concern to the Commission and is discussed in detail in Chapter 9.4.

3.7   Duties of the Managers under the Act - Section 23

The Managers under the Act are clearly defined in the Act itself. Many of their functions can be delegated to officers. However, the power to review detention or authorise discharge of a patient may not be delegated. All hospitals, and most private Registered Mental Nursing Homes, now conform to the relevant guidance in the Code of Practice. An error in the NHS and Community Care Act 1990 resulted in a situation in which the power to discharge patients under Section 23 could only be exercised by non-executive directors of a Trust. Unlike the situation with Health Authorities, it was not permissible to delegate this responsibility to a sub-committee of non-board members. This caused major problems in many areas. The situation has now been corrected by the Mental Health (Amendment) Act 1994. Trusts can now appoint sub-committees of informed independent persons.

The number of reviews held by Managers is very low in some areas and in some Registered Mental Nursing Homes (Chapter 9.7).

3.8   Consent to Treatment.

A more detailed discussion of this subject is given in Chapter 5. There has been a general improvement in practice but there are still many Forms 38 which are not completed in accordance with the advice given in the Code of Practice. There are some isolated examples of bad practice with no Forms 38 or 39 available and others where regularly used 'as required' (prn) medication is not included on Form 38. There are very few hospitals visited where the Forms 38 all comply with advice in the Code of Practice.

Not infrequently, members of the Commission find inadequate documentation in medical notes of attempts by RMOs to obtain informed consent to treatment from detained patients before treatment is given (Code of Practice 16.4) although there are some excellent examples of good practice in this respect. There is some concern that the provisions of the Act, as it stands, allow prolonged treatment without consent or a second medical opinion in a few cases where relatively prolonged periods of detention under the Act, each of less than three months duration, are interrupted by brief periods of discharge from detention.

Although neither the Act nor the Code of Practice gives precise guidance about the timing of reviews of treatment, the Mental Health Act Commission considers it good practice to review treatment plans regularly (Code of Practice 16.20) and to renew the certificate validating formal consent to treatment (Form 38) when the Section is renewed.

3.9   Seclusion.

The overall use of seclusion on open wards has declined to relatively low levels. It is more frequently employed in high dependency units and Special Hospitals but to a decreasing extent. In most cases, its use is in accordance with the Code of

Practice but the frequency of use in some units specialising in learning disability or acquired brain injury has been the cause of some concern. The Mental Health Act Commission has a clear and consistent view that any use of seclusion which is not in accordance with the Code of Practice is unacceptable. This is discussed in more detail under 'hospital issues' in Chapter 9.5.

3.10   Discharge Care Planning - Section 117

Section 117 of the Mental Health Act places a duty on health and local authorities to provide, in conjunction with relevant voluntary agencies, aftercare services for any patient who has been detained for treatment (Section 3), under a hospital order (Section 37) or transferred from prison (Sections 47 or 48) and ceases to be detained and leaves hospital.

The proper implementation of Section 117 of the Act is still patchy and is poor in some areas but, in others, a number of improved formats for Section 117 meetings have been introduced based on advice in the Code of Practice.

One of the most frequent criticisms made by visiting teams of Commission members is that discharge care planning does not begin early enough after admission to hospital. Section 117 meetings are often held at the last moment, sometimes after discharge and it is often not viewed as a priority by consultants. In practice, the documentation in relation to Section 117 often appears to be incorporated into that for the Care Programme Approach but patients subject to Section 117 aftercare are still usually easily identifiable within this system.

Many hospitals leave Section 117 planning until just before discharge, even when a Mental Health Review Tribunal hearing is imminent. In the event of discharge of the patient, it is clear that in such cases there would have been inadequate planning. The Commission recommends that the Section 117 planning commences soon after admission to hospital, although more detailed planning may await the time when discharge is foreseeable, either through a review hearing or because of improvement in the clinical state of the patient.

Some amendment to the Code of Practice on this matter would be helpful, since Department of Health guidelines (HC89(5), (referred to in HSG 94(27)), give detailed guidance on such planning and on those who should be involved. The guideline states "It is particularly important, as stays in hospital become shorter, that patients discharged back into the community should receive appropriate care. Planning should begin at an early stage and involve, where appropriate, the primary health care team, local authority social services and others. *For non-*

emergency cases where it is known that support will be required on discharge, planning should start before admission. For emergency cases it should start as soon as possible after admission. Lack of early and effective planning for services required after discharge can lead to "blocked beds" and unplanned readmission to hospital.". The guidance requires District and Special Health Authorities to ensure that proper procedures should be set in place with appropriate monitoring and report back.

3.11 Transfer to Hospital under Section 47 and 48.

Sentenced or remand prisoners, under certain circumstances, may be "removed to and detained in such hospital (not being a mental nursing home)". The Act does not authorise such transfers to Registered Mental Nursing Homes. This restriction clearly predates the increasing use of Registered Mental Nursing Homes to provide a large and important proportion of care in a secure or semi-secure environment and creates a number of difficulties in legally effecting the transfer. The Code of Practice gives no clear guidance and this item deserves some reconsideration when the Act is next revised. In the meantime, some clear guidance from the Department of Health would be welcomed.

3.12 The Police and Mental Health - Section 136

Section 136 empowers police officers to remove mentally disordered persons from a public place to a place of safety. Practice in the use of this Section has improved in most areas, with new jointly agreed policies, improved police awareness and training (see Chapter 8.2), and improved recording of its use.

In some places, however, matters are less satisfactory and the situation will be actively monitored by Commission members on visits.

> *Blackpool Wyre & Fylde Community Health Services NHS Trust* - *use of Section 36*
>
> *Members of the Commission have expressed concern over the level of confusion in the implementation of Section 136 in North Lancashire, which may be exacerbated by the existence of three alternative places of safety - the A & E dept, some police stations and acute psychiatric wards. The Commission questions the use of acute psychiatric wards as places of safety, as it could imply that a decision to admit a patient has been improperly made before assessment. The Commission also notes the lack of an agreed timescale for assessment, which has led to patients who were taken to psychiatric wards as a place of safety having to wait for an assessment until the following day. The Commission suggests that timescales should be included in Section 136 policies. Many areas have, for example, a six-hour waiting time before assessment.*

3.13   Validity of Faxed Forms

The Commission has been asked for its opinion on the validity of faxed forms. Although guidance is not given in the Code of Practice and this issue is not covered in the Act, Richard Jones in The Mental Health Act Manual (1994, 4th Edn London, Sweet and Maxwell, pp292) gives the view, which the Commission accepts, that faxed forms are acceptable. However, this view has not been the subject of a Court Judgement.

4 *Complaints*

Introduction

The investigation of complaints in all organisations, particularly in public services, has become increasingly important. This change has been promoted by the Citizen and Patient Charter initiatives, both of which have emphasised that effective handling of complaints is a key measure of the performance of public services. The implementation of the recommendations of the Wilson Review into NHS Complaints Procedures, published in May 1994, will give further impetus to this process. The Commission has similarly been concerned to improve the quality and efficacy of its complaints investigations and to respond to the criticisms made by the Ashworth Inquiry of its performance of this function. Through the investigation of complaints, the Commission has been able to highlight important areas of concern which are then monitored by Commission members on subsequent visits; some of these concerns are illustrated in the examples in this chapter. The importance to the Commission of its complaints jurisdiction is reflected by the appointment on 1 August 1995 of a Complaints Co-ordinator in the Nottingham Office; the aim is to systematise the response to complaints and to improve the overall quality of investigations.

4.1 The Commission's Complaints Remit

The Commission's jurisdiction to investigate complaints is set out in Section 120(1)(b) of the Mental Health Act 1983.

This section of the Act defines two types of complaints which the Commission may investigate:

- any complaint made by a person in respect of a matter which occurred while he was detained under the Act, and which has not been dealt with to his satisfaction by the Managers of a hospital or Registered Mental Nursing Home;
- any other complaint as to the exercise of powers and discharge of duties conferred or imposed by the Act in respect of a detained patient.

The Commission need not investigate a complaint within its jurisdiction and may discontinue an investigation where it is considered appropriate to do so. Where the Commission undertakes an investigation, a Commission member is entitled to visit and interview any patient and inspect any records relating to that person's detention or care. The Act obliges the Commission to report the findings of an investigation only in cases where the complaint has been made by a Member of Parliament.

4.2   The Processing of Complaints

The majority of complaints are in the form of letters to the Commission Office. Others are brought to the attention of Commission members on visits. Those which cannot be resolved satisfactorily during the course of that visit are then referred to the Commission Office. Many 'complaints' are, in fact, requests for information and much Secretariat and Commission member time is spent responding to these and referring them, where appropriate, to relevant organisations for assistance.

The majority of complaints fall under Section 120(1)(b)(i), i.e. they are matters which concern treatment and care rather than the exercise of powers and discharge of duties under the Act. This subsection authorises the Commission to undertake an investigation only after the complaint has been investigated by the Hospital Managers. In this sense the Commission's complaints jurisdiction provides a form of 'appeal' from a hospital or Trust's internal investigation. Many complainants do not appreciate this and refer complaints directly to the Commission. The Commission cannot investigate such complaints and fulfils a post-box function by referring the complainant back to the Hospital Managers. This is a time-wasting diversion for the complainant and the Commission is currently developing information leaflets for them which will set out clearly the procedures which should be followed.

Where the complaint concerns the exercise of powers or discharge of duties under the Act, the Commission may investigate without requiring the complainant to take the matter up with the hospital managers beforehand. In practice, however, it is usual for the Commission to seek a response from the hospital before deciding whether to conduct its own investigations.

The Commission has a policy and procedure for the investigation of complaints which outlines the Commission's objectives in relation to complaints investigations (Appendix 8.4). Within the last two years a comprehensive handbook on the investigation of complaints has been produced for use by both staff and Commission members.

The Mental Health Act does not define the circumstances in which the Commission may decline to investigate a complaint or to discontinue an investigation which has commenced. Important factors include the quality of investigation by the Hospital Managers, the accessibility of evidence relating to the events pertaining to the complaint (e.g. time that has elapsed, availability of witnesses) and the seriousness of the issues. In reviewing the investigation by the hospital managers, the Commission may take further steps which do not amount to a full investigation but nevertheless extend the enquiries relating to the complaint. For example, the Commission may ask the Managers to provide a complainant with access to his/her health records so that the matter may be clarified.

Some very thorough investigations undertaken by Hospital Managers are not reflected in the quality of response to the complainants. Complainants are often informed of the conclusions of an investigation and are assured that the process has been a thorough one without being told what records were seen, who was interviewed, the limits of the available information etc. It is hardly surprising that complainants remain dissatisfied and seek further investigation of their complaints. Thus the Commission may ask a hospital to elaborate its findings or to copy a witness statement to a complainant rather than undertake any further investigation.

Where the Commission undertakes a full investigation, it may examine medical, nursing and social services records and interview the complainant and other persons concerned. Almost invariably, the Commission provides a written report to the complainant which is copied to the Trust and/or persons concerned.

A major concern has been the variation between investigating Commission members in the quality and extent of the investigations they undertook. The appointment of the Complaints Co-ordinator should address this problem. The Co-ordinator will have overall responsibility for overseeing the Commission's complaints remit, including the development of Commission policy in this area. The Complaints Co-ordinator will be supported by a small geographically based team of Investigating Commission members who will have the responsibility for undertaking the necessary fieldwork in cases where the Co-ordinator feels that it is appropriate for it to carry out its own investigation into the concerns which have been raised.

At the same time, the Commission secretariat will have a small number of dedicated staff with the specific task of screening the complaints when they are first received and of providing the administrative support for full Commission investigations. The greater specialisation amongst both staff and Commission members, together with enhanced training, should result in improved performance in the way the Commission handles its complaints investigations.

4.3 Complaints Statistics

A summary of the Commission's statistics in relation to complaints is included at Appendix 9. In the period 1 July 1993 to 30 June 1995, the Commission dealt with 572 complaints through its formal Complaints Policy and Procedure (Appendix 8). In addition, it responded to 1568 "grievances". Complaints and grievances are received from many patients, relatives, health professionals and others. Many were referred back to Hospital Managers for investigation, after which the complainant did not pursue the matter. The number of full investigations undertaken by the Commission following the conclusion of a hospital investigation is small. The most common complaint over the past two years has been in the category of "offences against the person".

4.4 Complaints in Registered Mental Nursing Homes

The Commission has expressed its concerns about the quality of complaints investigations in medium secure Registered Mental Nursing Homes and has suggested the need for independent investigation of serious complaints. The Commission has undertaken a number of full investigations of complaints made by patients detained in these units.

The complaints in mental nursing homes often relate to poor patient-staff interaction, the use of control and restraint techniques, seclusion, the distance from home, family and friends and, at St Andrew's Hospital, the behavioural regime.

The Commission has been concerned about the way in which complaints are dealt with by the hospitals. Patients at one private Registered Mental Nursing Home have advised that they have little confidence in the complaints system. Complaint investigations are carried out by the hospital senior managers and it is rare for a complaint to be found in favour of the patient. Though the investigation of complaints is in line with NHS Trust practice, the Commission recommends that for serious incident inquiries the hospitals should consider bringing in an independent investigator, as occurs in the Special Hospitals. Current complaint policies should be reviewed in line with the Wilson recommendations for the review of NHS complaints procedures.

The Commission also recommends that Health Commissioning Agencies should monitor serious complaint inquiries that relate to those for whom they are purchasing care. The Commission at times has copied complaints to purchasers. This action has received positive support and has brought about a direct improvement for the patient.

4.5   Complaints in Special Hospitals

The Commission's complaints jurisdiction applies to all detained patients including those in Special Hospitals. However, the complaints procedures developed by the Special Hospitals include a system for internal 'appeal' to the Hospital Advisory Committee as well as referral to an independent investigator for certain categories of complaint. The Commission monitors the progress of such complaints and will undertake investigations when these procedures are exhausted. The consequence has been that the Commission undertakes relatively few full complaints investigations within the Special Hospitals. However, through its monitoring role, the Commission has identified aspects which require investigation by the Managers and this has resulted in a more satisfactory outcome for the patient. In one instance, a patient alleged that she had been assaulted by a member of the nursing staff. Commission members interviewed the patient and patients who were witnesses two days after the alleged assault and referred the matter to the hospital's Complaints Manager. The case was subsequently referred to an independent investigator who upheld the patient's complaint of assault. The investigator commented that the alleged degree of force used had probably been exaggerated by the patient witnesses and that different staff witnesses gave discrepant evidence. The investigator made no specific recommendations but the relevant member of staff was subsequently moved to another ward where his professional performance was monitored.

4.6   Complaints about the Mental Health Act Commission, Commission Members and SOADs

The Commission has a procedure for investigating complaints about Commission members. During the last two years 3 complaints resulted in an investigation in accordance with this procedure. They concerned:

- the fairness and accuracy of the Commission's feedback report following a Trust visit
- alleged failure to discuss with a consultant serious concerns that visiting Commission members had about the lawfulness of a patient's detention before taking further action on the patient's case

- confusion and delay in responding to a relative's concerns regarding a detained patient.

All the complaints were upheld in part and resulted in apologies to the complainants and a review of the relevant procedures and practices. A further complaint about the Commission was made to the Health Service Commissioner.

The Commission also has a procedure for investigating complaints about SOADs; most of these related to a shortfall in the consultation process. See Appendix 8.6 for details.

4.7   The Commission and the Health Service Commissioner

The Commission liaises with the Health Service Commissioner's office on a regular basis. The Commission was grateful to the Health Service Commissioner's office for participating in a training event on complaints at the Commission conference held in April 1994. The Health Service Commissioner has also agreed to assist in the training of the new complaints investigators.

There is an overlap in complaints jurisdiction between the two bodies who have agreed that, because of the Commission's expertise, complaints concerning detained patients should be investigated by the Commission in the first instance.

However, patients retain the right to complain to the Health Service Commissioner about the way the Commission has exercised its complaints jurisdiction. In the last two years one complaint against the Commission was adjudicated by the Health Service Commissioner.

The complainant, via a Community Health Council, complained to the unit in which he had been detained about various aspects of his care. He was satisfied with the unit's response except in respect of his complaint about the way he had been restrained by a member of the nursing staff. This matter was referred to the Commission. Some two months later, the Commission informed the Community Health Council that, it its view, an investigation by the Commission would be unlikely to provide any further information and that it was satisfied that the unit had investigated the matter adequately. The patient complained to the Health Service Commissioner that the Commission's decision not to investigate had neither been reached with sufficient urgency nor with appropriate thoroughness and impartiality because of its reliance upon the information obtained from the unit's investigation.

The Health Service Commissioner concluded that the case should have been dealt with more speedily and, whilst the Commission had not displayed partiality or lack of integrity, it should have appraised more critically the results of the hospital investigation. The Commissioner suggested that the Commission should have probed the reliability of the information on which the Managers' investigation was based. It should also have sent a more detailed final response to the complainant - a criticism that the Health Service Commissioner had made in respect of an earlier adjudication concerning the Commission (reported in the Fifth Biennial Report Chapter 6.5). The Commission accepted these criticisms and apologised to the patient.

4.8 Implications of the Wilson Review of NHS Complaints Procedures

From April 1996, the recommendations of the Wilson Committee, which reviewed NHS complaints procedures, will be implemented. They will introduce a two-tier process for dealing with complaints within the health service. There will be internal investigations followed, if necessary, by reference to an independent review panel.

In terms of the proposed procedures, the Commission understands that a Commissioner would be co-opted on to a review panel where a complaint concerns a detained patient. While the Commission would welcome this role it believes that detained patients should retain the right to ask the Commission to investigate a matter relating to their treatment and care and the operation of the Act. Complaints remain an important source of information to the Commission about the operation of the Act and the care of patients and it is essential that that source is not lost. In its response to the Wilson Review, the Commission suggested that it should retain its power to investigate complaints but that its remit should be amended to give it greater discretion as to which issues it may investigate.

The Commission was pleased to note that the report recognises the difficulty of access for people with mental health problems. However, the proposed changes do not address the main problems that many mentally ill people experience, particularly that their complaints are frequently seen as a symptom of their illness. In addition, there are patients who have a valid cause for complaint but because of their mental condition are unable to realise this. The Commission expressed its concern that, without some specific provision for people with mental health problems, their complaints may not be made, or will be unjustifiably screened out at an early stage.

4.9   Examples of Commission Complaints Investigations

A substantial number of complaints received each year are made by the relatives of patients who have died while detained under the Act. Such complaints fall within Section 120(1)(b)(ii) of the Act (see above) with the result that the Commission can only investigate those complaints which concern the exercise of powers and discharge of duties under the Act. Some of these cascs raise very important issues about the quality of care which fall outside the Commission's complaints jurisdiction e.g. inadequate staffing levels, failure to follow observation guidelines, inadequate resuscitation facilities etc. Although the Commission's narrow jurisdiction is explained to complainants, the subsequent investigation of powers and duties is a disappointment and, understandably, regarded as failing to address the vital issues associated with the patient's death.

For the same reason, the Commission is unable to investigate an allegation of assault against a patient unless the patient is willing and able to make that complaint. This leaves the most vulnerable and disabled patients further disadvantaged.

Case study 1 illustrates this issue and also highlights the importance of developing sound policies in relation to the granting of Section 17 leave - an issue that seriously concerned the Robinson inquiry. Case 2 is an investigation into the circumstances of a patient's transfer from one hospital to another under Section 19 of the Act. Both complaints were raised by relatives in respect of patients who died and both concerned the exercise of powers and/or discharge of duties under the Act. Although there is no requirement in such cases that the complaint should be made to the Managers in the first place, in both instances the Commission sought the Managers' comments before deciding to undertake a further investigation.

Case study 3 concerns an allegation by a patient of racial abuse and illustrates the difficulties in investigating complaints by patients concerning the actions of staff. Case 4 concerns both issues of good practice and of law in making an application by a Nearest Relative; it also illustrates the need for the proper maintenance of patient records.

CASE STUDY 1

The Complaint

*   The complainant was the mother of a patient who died while detained under

Section 3 of the Act. The patient had failed to return from authorised leave and had been found dead some days later. The mother alleged that:

- he should not have been granted leave under Section 17;
- the hospital failed to take the necessary steps to return him to hospital when he was absent without leave under Section 18;
- the relatives were misinformed as to his whereabouts and only belatedly informed about his death;
- generally the relatives were treated insensitively.

The complainants were informed that, because of jurisdiction limitations noted above, only the first two allegations could be investigated.

The Hospital Managers' Response

The complainant had raised her case with her MP, who had received from the hospital a detailed account of the circumstances of the death. According to that account, the patient's clinical condition had improved sufficiently to allow the granting of periods of leave; further that he often failed to return in time and that this was not a reason for undue alarm. The hospital acknowledged in general terms that the procedures for granting leave and monitoring absences should be tightened up, although no specific problems were identified.

The complainant was not satisfied with this response.

The Commission's Investigation

The Commission examined a report to the Coroner from the patient's RMO, a report by a Commissioner who attended the inquest into the patient's death, the patient's health records including both medical and nursing notes from the time of his admission to his death and statements by members of the clinical staff concerning the events immediately before his death.

The Commission's Findings

The Commission found serious gaps in the procedures for authorising Section 17 leave. In particular, it found that leave had, on occasions, been granted by persons other than the patient's RMO; that the accounts of his leave status were confused and that nursing and medical records did not concur; that there was no record of the clinical team's decision not to restrict the patient's pass in view of his 'abuse' of it, nor any decision regarding the circumstances when the missing persons procedure should be invoked and that Section 17 leave forms were not in use. On the other hand, the Commission concluded that the granting of leave was justified in view of his apparent clinical improvement and that the decision not to immediately invoke the missing persons procedure was reasonable in view of his past behaviour.

Further Action

The details of this investigation were passed to the visiting team who were able to monitor the procedures for granting leave on subsequent visits. Section 17 forms were devised and although their use was patchy at first, it is now much improved. The hospital issued an additional policy concerning the procedure for alerting the police when patients abscond.

CASE STUDY 2

The Complaint

The complaint was made by the sister of a patient who had died following his transfer from a Regional Secure Unit (RSU) to a Special Hospital. The patient had been physically unwell prior to transfer and, on arrival at the Special Hospital, was immediately referred to a general hospital. He was subsequently found to have suffered multiple cerebral infarcts and died 3 months later. The complainant alleged that her brother had been medically unfit for transfer and that the authority to transfer him under Section 19 should not have been given by the RSU.

The Hospital Managers' Response

A detailed explanation of the events leading to the patient's death was given to the complainant by the unit's Service Manager. He stated that, although there was concern about the patient's condition before his transfer, there was no medical evidence to suggest that, 'on balance', the transfer should not proceed. He added that it had been thought that the patient's anxiety about the impending transfer was contributing to his physical state.

The Commission's Investigation

The Commission examined the health records relating to the patient's stay at the RSU, his brief admission to the Special Hospital and his subsequent transfer to the general hospital. It sought and obtained further information from the Service Manager, the patient's RMOs at the RSU and at the Special Hospital and an ENT specialist who had examined the patient briefly on the morning of his transfer. Two medical members of the Commission independently reviewed the health records.

The Commission's Findings

The Commission found that, despite the deterioration in the patient's physical state and the concern about this expressed by his relatives and nursing staff on the night before his transfer, there was no evidence that a full physical examination had been done before his transfer. It appeared that the RSU staff considered that the patient's condition was psychogenic in origin, relating to his anxiety about the transfer. The Commission upheld this complaint.

Further Action

In response to this incident the Trust introduced a new policy on the transfer of patients which required patients to undergo a physical examination before transfer. On the Commission's suggestion, the policy also required receiving staff to be alerted to any concerns about a patient's health and that relevant nursing and medical notes should accompany the patient.

CASE STUDY 3

The Complaint

The patient alleged that two members of the nursing staff had made racist remarks by saying that he looked like another patient's toy ape.

The Hospital Managers' Investigation

The Managers obtained the views of the two nursing staff against whom the allegation was made. They attempted to talk to the complainant but he refused to speak to them.

The Managers concluded that the complainant had misinterpreted the remarks made by the staff as applying to him, rather than to the toy. The complainant was not satisfied.

The Commission's Investigation

The investigating Commissioner interviewed the complainant, 5 patients whom the complainant regarded as possible witnesses to the event and 3 members of staff including the two accused. The Commissioner also examined the patient's health records.

The Findings

One of the patients was able to recall the incident, as did the two accused members of staff. The Commission member concluded that the event recalled by the complainant probably did take place and that, although the staff's reactions were not intended to be racist, they were open to that misinterpretation. The Commissioner recommended that all staff are given race-awareness training. Criticism was also made about the quality of the hospital's investigation in failing to attempt to identify any independent witnesses to the alleged incident.

Case Study 4

The Complaint

The complaint was made by a patient who had been detained by virtue of an application by his father as statutory Nearest Relative. The complainant, supported by his father, alleged that :

- his father was improperly pressured by clinical staff to apply for his son's admission and that this had had serious consequences for their subsequent relationship;

- he was denied access to an independent second opinion as to the nature of his illness.

The second complaint was subsequently discontinued because the nursing notes relating to the relevant period were missing from the health records.

The Hospital Managers' Response

Neither the patient's RMO nor the Hospital Managers were able to explain why the application was not made by an Approved Social Worker. They acknowledged that Nearest Relative applications were highly unusual. The patient's RMO insisted that, while he had persuaded the complainant's father not to oppose the application, he had not asked him to sign the application.

The Commission's Investigation

The Commission examined the available health records (much of the nursing record was missing) and legal documentation, interviewed the complainant and his RMO, obtained a statement from a family friend of the complainant who had accompanied the father to the hospital during the relevant period and from the patient's father and had further correspondence with the relevant Social Services Department, the hospital's Chief Executive, the duty registrar at the time of admission and the duty administrator.

The Commission's Findings

Because of the missing health records and the time that had elapsed since the events complained of, the Commission was unable to determine why the complainant's father, rather than an ASW, had made the application. However, the patient was detained under Section 5(2) at the time of the application and there was no apparent reason why the application could not have awaited the availability of an ASW on the following day. In view of the guidance given in the Code of Practice that the Nearest Relative should be advised 'that it is preferable for an ASW to make an assessment of the need for a patient to be admitted under the Act, and for the ASW to make the application' (para 2.30), the Commission upheld the complaint. It also found that the hospital had failed to fulfil its statutory duty under Section 14 to request a report from Social Services following the Nearest Relative application. It recommended that Nearest Relative applications are monitored and that the hospital's information recording and retrieval systems should be overhauled.

Further Action

The Commission intends to monitor this situation on subsequent visits to the Trust.

5 Treatment, Medication and Consent

Introduction

The Commission is responsible for the administration of the Consent to Treatment provisions of Part IV of Mental Health Act. As part of this remit, it appoints registered medical practitioners as Second Opinion Appointed Doctors (SOADs) to validate treatment plans when detained patients are not consenting to medical treatment after a period of three months from the first prescription of medication during a period of continuous detention, or for the administration of ECT at any time. SOADs, and other persons who are not medical practitioners, are also appointed for treatments falling within the provisions of Section 57 (pertaining to psychosurgery and the implantation of hormones). The Commission routinely inspects treatment plans and consent certification on its visits to hospitals.

5.1   Treatment Requiring Consent and a Second Opinion

Referrals under Section 57

All referrals of patients to the Commission under Section 57 were for psychosurgery.   There were no referrals for hormone implantation. Most psychosurgical operations continued to be undertaken in the Geoffrey Knight Unit at Brook Hospital in London. Further information is given in Appendix 4.1.

Form 37 (Authorisation Form)

The Commission-appointed doctors undertaking Section 57 visits have been advised to set a time limit on the validity of Form 37, i.e. stating that the certificate "remains valid for only 8 weeks from the date of this certificate". It remains the view of the Commission as stated in its Fifth Report that a new Form 37 would be necessary if an operation was postponed for more than 8 weeks after certification. Consent of the patient to treatment is essential for a certificate to be issued.

Consultation Problems

Problems have occurred in the certification process when:

- the doctor who made the referral to the operation centre was no longer the patient's psychiatrist;

- "the other professional" had been recruited specifically to satisfy the statutory requirement and appeared not to be genuinely professionally concerned with the patient's medical treatment and unlikely to be involved in aftercare;

- the consultation procedure took place almost immediately prior to a scheduled operation date;

- there was a lack of awareness of procedure involved in Section 57 consultation although these are outlined very clearly in Chapter 16 of the Code of Practice.

After Care Arrangements

The importance of adequate aftercare arrangements has been emphasised in a number of recent publications and particular attention is paid to this aspect of care by the Commission-appointed teams. Aftercare arrangements cannot be properly evaluated in the case of referrals from overseas, but there are also occasional problems with referrals from within the United Kingdom.

Analysis of Section 61 Reports

The Commission has a monitoring role in relation to psychosurgery and asks for a Section 61 report on the patient's progress. It is desirable that this report should incorporate the patient's view of their progress but this does not always occur. Further progress reports may be requested as considered appropriate in each individual case. (see Appendix 4.1 for statistical information)

Evaluation of "perceived outcome" is inevitably subjective and any impression of a patient's view of the operation has to be seen in the context of a report submitted by the consultant rather than information supplied directly by the patient. The figures below do not represent a definitive, qualitative study of the outcome of psychosurgery, but rather an attempt, using the information available, to evaluate and identify distinctive trends and features. Considerable caution is therefore necessary in any interpretation.

	Outcome Perceived by:	
	RMO	Patient
Significant Improvement	9	7
Some Improvement	17	12
No Change	6	11
Some Deterioration	1	0
Significant Deterioration	1	0
Total	34	30

In four cases the views of the patient were not known. It was noted in two of the cases monitored that the patients experienced significant personality changes following the operation.

Information Leaflet

A leaflet is currently being prepared in order to help patients, relatives and staff understand the consent procedures governing neurosurgery for mental disorder and the role of the Mental Health Act Commission in relation to the certification of consent.

5.2   Treatment Requiring Consent or a Second Opinion
- Section 58

Appointment of Second Opinion Appointed Doctors (SOADs) and training

Revised procedures for the appointment of Section 58 Appointed Doctors have been implemented, involving more vigorous selection and re-appointment procedures. New SOADs have attended monitoring sessions as well as the series of SOAD seminars held in York, Meriden and Bristol. The general discussions have been enlivened by presentations from senior nurses and others involved in the consultation process.

Monitoring

Further efforts have been made to systematically review the reports completed by SOADs, which contain a wealth of significant clinical data, and the copies of the relevant consent to treatment certificate, Form 39 (now routinely submitted by SOADs). This task is undertaken monthly by members of the Commission, assisted by Commission staff. While the responsibility for the certificate rests with each SOAD, the Commission draws attention to obvious deficiencies in certification and provides feedback on a standard form, noting significant errors. This information is reviewed by the Commission when appointments or re-appointments are considered. The large number of reports and forms received at present results in less attention being given to this task than is desirable, especially as the Commission gives priority to the review of reports submitted to it when treatment is reviewed under the provisions of Section 61.

The Commission has not been able to distinguish between the cancellation of SOAD visits by the hospital, without informing the Commission, and the failure to submit reports by the SOAD. This has led to a discrepancy between the number of Second Opinions requested under Section 58 and the number of reports received. This failure to notify cancellations has caused considerable work for

Commission staff. The Commission is currently investigating alternative arrangements for the monitoring of these reports.

Guidance to SOADs

New guidance has been issued, which clarifies certain matters not available in the Code of Practice.

Agreement between the Section 58 Appointed Doctor and the Responsible Medical Officer

A revised report form has been introduced which requires information on the extent to which the treatment plan has been modified by the intervention of the Section 58 Appointed Doctor.

Statistical Information regarding Section 58

Detailed information is given in Appendix 4.2.

- **Category of disorder**

The overwhelming majority, 93%, of all Second Opinion visits were for the category of mental illness. The figures were 3.7% for mental impairment, 1.7% for severe mental impairment and 1.6% for psychopathic disorder. However, there were some interesting regional differences. In two Regional Health Authorities, East Anglia and Northern, there was 8.9% and 9.5% referrals, respectively, for mental impairment. In Oxford and Yorkshire it was 5.3% and 4.9% respectively, whereas in all other authorities the percentage was less than 3%. Among Special Hospitals, Rampton Hospital had 18% referrals for mental impairment, whereas Ashworth Hospital and Broadmoor Hospital were both below 3%, possibly reflecting the greater intake of mentally impaired patients into Rampton Hospital.

Ashworth Hospital stands alone in the high percentage of referrals regarding patients with a diagnosis of psychopathic disorder. This percentage is 17% of all referrals, greater than either of the other two Special Hospitals.

- **Gender differences in the use of ECT**

Seventy percent of all referrals for a statutory Second Opinion for ECT treatment were for female patients. In contrast, the majority (64%) of referrals regarding medication were for men. These differences may, in part, be attributable to differences in ages and diagnoses between male and female patients.

5.3   Out of Hours Visits

Some of the difficulties which SOADs face in consulting a third person, as required by the Act, arise from Second Opinion visits made outside normal working hours.

The Commission tries to ensure that the list of doctors available for appointment to an individual patient who requires a Second Opinion includes as many doctors in active clinical practice as possible. These Consultants are less available during normal working hours than recently retired consultants. However, the Commission is anxious not to depend too heavily on medical practitioners who may be perceived as out of touch with clinical practice. In fact, the Commission has relied on a number of senior, respected and very well informed Second Opinion Appointed Doctors for some years. These SOADs have had unique experience of seeing seriously ill patients requiring second opinions under the Act. A number of these practitioners were appointed to the Commission at its inception. As some doctors have now reached 70 years of age their appointments have not been renewed. They will be greatly missed and the Commission takes this opportunity to record its appreciation of their diligent and informed service as SOADs.

5.4   Information to Patients

The Commission published an information leaflet relating to Part IV of the Act in October 1994. An improved version of this is in preparation, as is a leaflet relating to psychosurgery under Section 57.

5.5   Treatment Plans

The Code of Practice (16.12) recommends for consenting patients that "the RMO should indicate on the certificate the drugs proposed by the classes described in the British National Formulary (BNF), the method of their administration and the dose range (indicating the dosages if they are above the BNF maximum advisory limits)." The Commission recommends that the maximum number of drugs in each BNF category should also be specified in the plan and on Form 39. At a plenary training session, the Commission considered the current guidance on the description of treatment within the treatment plan. The advantages of specifying medication in the terms recorded on the prescription, giving the drug name, route and dosage rather than the more general description using BNF categories was favoured by some but this would cause a loss of flexibility, would require more frequent renewal of Forms 38 validating the patients' consent and would generate more requests for Second Opinions. It was suggested that such a requirement would also provide greater safeguards for detained patients and this proposal will be kept under review.

The judgement of the General Medical Council, that an anaesthetist was guilty of serious professional misconduct by not securing a patient's consent to the use of an analgesic suppository during the course of a dental anaesthetic, serves to emphasise the importance of giving full and accurate information as to the nature, purpose and likely effects of treatment.

St Ann's Hospital (Haringey Health Trust) distributes useful guidance with their Forms 38. The guidance outlines the BNF categories of regularly and occasionally used drugs employed to treat mental illness, together with a reminder to stipulate the dosage limit agreed with the patient, e.g. "within BNF limits".

5.6 Recommended Dose Ranges and the British National Formulary

The Commission was represented on the Royal College of Psychiatrists (RCP) Working Party which considered the use of anti-psychotic drugs above the doses recommended for general use in the British National Formulary (BNF). Their report [9] indicates the safeguards which should be used when higher than usual doses are administered and gives a useful summary of the maximum daily doses for oral antipsychotics and depot injections. The report has been welcomed and is now referred to in the latest edition of the British National Formulary. The report has been circulated to all SOADs and discussed at SOAD seminars, at which the Chairman of the Working Group, Professor C Thompson, gave an address on this topic. The Commission appreciates the time and trouble which Professor Thompson took to ensure that the guidance of the College was brought to the attention of the Appointed Doctors.

While the Commission's recording procedure asks SOADs to identify the use of higher than BNF doses and ECT courses which exceed 12 treatments, the Commission itself does not determine the treatment to be given, as this is a matter for the professional judgement of the RMO and the Appointed Doctor.

On occasions, the Commission has been contacted by hospitals requesting a Second Opinion for patients receiving doses above BNF limits either within the three months period or on the basis of the patients' valid consent. These requests represent a misunderstanding of the statutory provisions, which leaves decisions regarding dosages to the clinical judgement of the RMO. However, the Commission advises RMOs and SOADs that the upper limit should always be defined and that the phrase, "above BNF limits", without further specification, is not regarded as satisfactory.

5.7 Polypharmacy

When members of the Commission visit hospitals, they frequently observe simultaneous use of several antipsychotic drugs, often in large doses cumulatively above BNF limits. There may be sound reasons for administering more than one antipsychotic drug of the same type (to have a varying duration of action for example). However, with multiple drug administration, it becomes difficult to assess hazards associated with the combination and there may be a failure to appreciate that a combination of drugs from different BNF subcategories, such as 4.2.1 and 4.2.2, or a combination of 'as required' with regular administration will produce additive effects. The BNF gives approximate equivalent doses for oral antipsychotics and for depot preparations. The Consensus Report from the RCP gives maximum doses for oral antipsychotics and depot antipsychotic drugs and highlights the potential hazard from prescribing 'as required' drugs as oral or intramuscular, without specifying different doses by each route. Whilst the prescribing of drugs is clearly a matter of clinical judgement and the Commission does not give advice in such matters, it commends the BNF statement that "the prescribing of more than one antipsychotic drug at a time is not recommended; it may constitute a hazard and there is no significant evidence that the side-effects are minimised".

5.8   Covert Administration of Medication.

The Commission has been consulted on the acceptability, in exceptional circumstances, of the covert administration of medication to patients who are not consenting to treatment. For example, in order to enable medication to be given to an elderly, non-consenting patient, without danger to staff, the patient was given medication disguised in tea. The Commission fears that such practices may be widespread in many nursing homes which are not visited by the Commission, including some which take detained patients. Neither the Act itself nor the Code of Practice gives explicit guidance and the views of individual practitioners appear to vary. Some consider it unacceptable on the grounds that it would be difficult to assess the amount of medication actually taken, which could make the procedure potentially dangerous to the patient. Others feel that this method might be in the best interests of the patient. However, there is a general feeling that in most cases the technique would be employed for the convenience of staff rather than for the safety of the patient and would therefore be unacceptable.

One of the problems associated with covert administration is that it is clearly impossible to attempt to negotiate consent to such treatment and covert administration to a detained patient is seemingly precluded by para 16.11 in the Code of Practice and by Section 58 (3)a of the Act, unless it has been certified as acceptable by a Second Opinion Doctor under Section 58(3)b. In contrast, it has been argued that a doctor may be entitled to withhold information from the patient under para 15.13 of the Code but must be prepared to justify that decision. However, for that to be valid, the treatment must be "in accordance with practice accepted at the time by a responsible body of medical opinion skilled in the particular form of treatment in question" (Code of Practice para 15.19). It would seem appropriate therefore for this matter to be considered by the Royal College of Psychiatrists and the Royal College of Nursing. Meanwhile, professional judgement must be relied upon in making decisions on this important ethical issue.

5.9   Ethnic Monitoring

The new SOAD report form includes questions on the ethnic category of detained patients for whom compulsory treatment under the provisions of Section 58(3)(b) is requested.

5.10   'The Three Month Rule'

The three month period gives time for the doctor to create a treatment plan suitable for the patient's needs. Despite clear guidance (Code of Practice 16.11, 16.13: Commission Practice Note 2), it is a Commission finding that attempts to negotiate consent to treatment before the expiration of three months are not scrupulously recorded in the medical notes. This is particularly important where there is prolonged, continuous, treatment in hospital amounting to more, maybe much more, than three months in duration, with periods of detention under the Act each of less than three months but separated by short intervals of informal status. This part of the Code of Practice needs to be re-evaluated to take account of this situation (see also Chapter 3, Code of Practice).

5.11   Review of Treatment - Section 61

A new Section 61 report form has been introduced, which includes explanatory notes drawn from the Code of Practice. When used, this report form is very helpful to the Commission in determining whether a further second opinion should be arranged. Unfortunately there remain many occasions when old forms are used or reports are made without the data being completed. This arises in part from the relatively few occasions on which reports under this Section are required, since most detained patients (outside the Special Hospitals) are either consenting to treatment or are recovered and discharged when renewal of section would be due.

5.12   Scrutiny of Documents and Renewal of Consent to Treatment Forms (Form 38)

The revised Code of Practice has been helpful in relation to the scrutiny of documents and in clarifying aspects of the treatment plan, for example, the specification of the dose range. Some further guidance is necessary in relation to the duration of consent to treatment certificates issued by the RMO (Form 38). The Commission has suggested that the form certifying the validity of the patient's consent should always be renewed by the RMO if there is a permanent change of RMO, a significant change of treatment or a break in the continuity of detention. However, it is also considered to be good practice if these forms are renewed at the times specified for the reports under Section 61, i.e. at the time of renewal of detention. The Commission expects that the patient's consent status will be kept under close and regular review between such times, with appropriate records made as required by the Code of Practice.

The Commission guidance, given in the Fifth Biennial Report, that Form 38 should contain the words "This certificate renders earlier certificates null and void" has not been implemented. It is a fairly common finding that more than one consent to treatment form is in existence at the same time. The Commission recommends that a new form should be completed each time there is any change in the treatment plan which is not covered by an existing Form 38 and that obsolete forms should be struck through, but not destroyed, to avoid confusion.

5.13   The Third Consultee

There has been no resolution of the problems frequently reported by SOADs in relation to the identification and availability of the third consultee - who has to be neither a doctor nor a nurse. Indeed, as units become smaller and more scattered, there are increasing difficulties in maintaining multi-disciplinary working. The Commission has continued to receive certificates naming "the ward clerk" or the "ward domestic" as being professionally concerned in the patients' medical treatment as SOADs do their best to ensure that the patients' treatment is uninterrupted. This is an issue which lends itself to quality standards and purchasers should be encouraged to meet fully the statutory obligations which this part of the Act requires.

5.14   Emergency Treatment - Section 62

A practice note concerning Section 62 treatment together with a model form is being prepared by the Commission. It is hoped that this will reduce the confusion which still surrounds emergency treatment. This issue is of particular concern because of the anecdotal evidence that patients treated in emergency situations, often under Common Law and by inexperienced staff, are particularly subject to harm including collapse and death. This matter is considered in the Royal College of Psychiatrists guidelines on anti-psychotic medication and these should be drawn to the attention of casualty officers and any staff likely to be involved in emergency treatment situations.

5.15   Detained Patients on Extended Section 17 Leave

Some patients are sent from Special Hospitals to Medium Secure Units on extended leave under the provisions of Section 17. There is no provision for delegating the consent to treatment responsibilities of the RMO, yet the doctor actually in charge of the patient's ongoing treatment is the consultant in the receiving hospital. A similar situation may arise when patients are sent on extended Section 17 leave to their homes in the community, which may be a residential care home or other residence. This creates difficulties when changes in consent status or treatment require the completion of Forms 38 or 39 and infringes the concept of Section 17 leave. The Commission is seeking further clarification of the use of Section 17 leave in these situations (see also Chapter 4, Code of Practice).

5.16   The Incapable patient

A study on patients with dementia, many of whom are not liable to be detained under the Act, has been undertaken with respect to de facto detention and issues of consent. This is to be the subject of a Commission report.

5.17   Research on Detained Patients

A working group of the Commission has begun to consider the ethical implications of research being carried out on detained patients.

The Commission has, as yet, made no formal statement on this matter. However, it does seem clear that even if, for example, a detained patient consents to take part in a randomised drug trial, the consent to treatment provisions still apply, which may cause some difficulty. For example, during the initial three months periods of treatment whilst detained, the Code of Practice states (Para 16.11) that "the patient's RMO must ensure that the patient's valid consent is sought prior to the administration of any medication", and (para 16.13), "Although the patient can be treated in the absence of consent in this period no such treatment should be given in the absence of an attempt to gain valid consent".

Section 58(3)(a) requires that, after three months, the patient consents and that the RMO certifies that the patient is capable of understanding the nature, purpose, and likely effect of the treatment and has consented to it. The question arises as to whether such consent can be valid in a randomised drug trial when both the patient and the RMO are ignorant as to the precise nature of the medication being administered.

There is also a possible problem where placebo drugs are being administered when a patient is being detained for "treatment".

The Commission will consider issuing some guidance on these matters, but in the meantime would suggest that the involvement of detained patients in a study must primarily be the responsibility of the appropriate ethics committee.

5.18 Complaints in Relation to Part IV

The Commission monitors all the reports, and copies of Forms 39 which are completed and returned to the office by Second Opinion Appointed Doctors. Any deficiencies noted by the monitoring group are brought to the attention of the doctor concerned. There is therefore a high degree of quality control over this aspect of the Commission's activities. Nevertheless, the Commission does on occasion receive complaints in relation to the Second Opinion procedures. If these involve complaints about a SOAD, there is a formal policy and procedure within the Commission for dealing with such complaints (Appendix 8.6).
Bearing in mind the large number of Second Opinions processed, the number of complaints received is relatively small: Out of the 8 complaints received, one was upheld. Most of the complaints relate to what was perceived by the complainant to be a shortfall or defect in the consultation process.

6 *Inquests and Deaths of Detained Patients*

Introduction

The Commission's Fifth Biennial Report drew attention to the Commission's interest in the deaths of detained patients. The Commission requests all hospitals to notify deaths of detained patients direct to the Commission, and it has been the Commission's practice, wherever possible, to send a member of the Commission to attend inquests.

The primary reason for a member of the Commission to attend an inquest is to ascertain information which is relevant to the exercise of powers and duties under the Act, insofar as procedures or facilities for detained patients are defective or inadequate. The information gathered may be useful locally in that it may identify problems in a particular unit, or may contribute to the Commission's understanding of more wide-spread problems. The role of a Commission member at an inquest is primarily as an observer.

In its last Biennial Report the Commission reported on the recorded information on 143 inquests attended between 1991 and 1993. At the time of going to press on the Fifth Biennial Report a detailed analysis of the deaths of detained patients was not yet available. A full report has now been produced [10] and it makes a number of recommendations and highlights a number of shortcomings in the care of patients detained under the Mental Health Act.

6.1 Shortfalls in Procedures

One surprising finding from the study was the high proportion of mental health units which reported that they did not hold serious incident reviews after the unexpected death of a patient. The results demonstrate that there is an urgent need for service managers in many units to develop review procedures in line with the Department of Health guidelines. The draft guide to Arrangements for Interagency Working for the Care and Protection of the Severely Mentally Ill (Department of Health 1994) stressed the importance of units establishing procedures for local audit and serious incident reviews. Detailed guidance on the auditing of suicides and other serious incidents is contained in Clinical Audit of Suicide and other Unexpected Deaths (NHSE 1994). If such procedures are implemented, and lessons learned, a number of unexpected deaths could probably be prevented.

It was also clear that few mental health units currently have a risk management strategy designed to assist staff in the difficult job of assessing clinical risks. It is essential that the risks involved in managing detained patients are continually assessed. It is recommended that all mental health services should now have a clinical risk management policy.

Another worrying finding of the study was that a very high proportion of the deaths occurred after the patient absconded from hospital, usually within a few hours of leaving. Many of today's psychiatric units are old, and not designed for easy observation. The situation is not helped by the high numbers of very disturbed patients on the acute wards, which is very demanding for staff, particularly when minimum staffing levels are found in many hospitals.

In many units, policies allow a period of several hours to elapse before hospital grounds are searched, and relatives and police are alerted. The analysis revealed that over a third of patients who died after absconding did so within 6 hours, and half died within 12 hours. A significant number of lives might therefore have been saved if a search had been instituted straight away.

It was also found that a third of all patients who died did so whilst on authorised leave of absence from the hospital, which suggests that units should check that they have a policy for implementing Section 17 procedures, and all staff should be trained in its implementation (see also Chapter 9.4).

Some of the cases included in the study revealed a pattern of escalating quantities of mixed neuroleptics and other sedatives, large doses given intramuscularly every few hours, prescribed by junior doctors often with very little supervision. The overall impression from these inquest reports was of inexperienced nurses and junior doctors attempting to control a difficult and potentially dangerous patient outside normal working hours with a minimum of supervision. Very few psychiatric units have developed protocols for dealing with patients with severely disturbed behaviour. (See also Chapters 7 and 9).

6.2 Summary of Recommendations Arising out of the Report

- Mental health professionals should have training in the high risk of suicide among patients diagnosed as suffering from schizophrenia or a related disorder.

- All mental health units should have a clinical risk management policy.

- Units with a high level of absconding are advised to review the physical environment and care policies in the unit.

- The absence of patients who have absconded, or who have failed to return from leave at the agreed time, and have already been identified as suicide risks, should be notified immediately to the police and an immediate search should be made by unit staff.

- All units should ensure that staff are trained in the use of a Section 17 leave policy. The policy should conform to the guidelines in the Code of Practice (see also Chapters 3 and 9.4).

- All mental health units should have an agreed clinical protocol for the management of patients with seriously disturbed behaviour.

- The professionals involved in the care and treatment of patients who commit suicide should inform the Department of Health's Confidential Inquiry into Homicides and Suicides by Mentally Ill People (P.O. Box 1515, London SW1X 8PL).

The Commission is currently reviewing the way in which it collects information about the deaths of detained patients, and will continue to take a deep interest in this subject. The research summarised in this chapter illustrates what valuable lessons there are to be learned from a systematic review of patient deaths.

7 Special Patient Groups

7.1 Adolescents and Young People

Introduction

A number of units have provision to detain adolescents from time to time. However, the Commission has, in the last two years, had a particular interest in the Adolescent Forensic Psychiatry Services provided by Salford Mental Health Services at the Gardner Unit. This service offers a combination of facilities which provides in-patient assessment and treatment functions for adolescents within a medium level of security, combined with a community team which is able to offer local secondary level services and outreach workers from the in-patient unit.

The final summary report of the Review of Health and Social Services for Mentally Disordered Offenders (Reed Report, 1992 - Department of Health and Home Office) made several recommendations which apply to the type of services provided from the Gardner Unit.

The recommendations were that:

- *there should be research to establish the national prevalence of children requiring secure or related specialised services*
- *current levels of secure health provision for mentally disordered adolescents should at least be maintained, preferably through closer links with services provided by other agencies*
- *Regional Health Authorities, in conjunction with other agencies, should consider establishing small core teams which can provide advice and support to those caring for mentally disordered children and adolescents with specialised needs*
- *as far as possible specialised services for mentally disordered adolescents should be developed as part of a wider multi-agency service*
- *agencies should develop a joint approach to ensuring that adolescents with learning disabilities who offend or appear to be at risk of offending have*

access to a range of general and specialised services suitable for their age and stage of development and they do not get drawn unnecessarily into the criminal justice system.

The Commission urges the full implementation of these proposals and is concerned that there are still instances where adolescents are inappropriately placed in adult wards. The Commission is also aware of growing difficulties with young males, usually aged 17-20, with drug abuse problems who are increasingly being detained in mainstream psychiatric units.

The Use of Compulsory Admission

In February 1994, a review team published a report based on fieldwork undertaken at the Gardner Unit in November and December 1983. The review was carried out jointly by the Mental Health Act Commission, the Health Advisory Service and the Social Services Inspectorate.

Young people are either admitted to the unit under the authority of the Children's Act 1989 or the Mental Health Act 1983. The review team noted that the route by which a young person is detained appeared to be somewhat arbitrary in that there is no specific policy set out by the Health Authority, Salford Mental Health Services or the unit. In general the route of admission was dictated by the referring Authority.

There is a debate about the desirability of using mental health legislation because of the stigma of compulsory admission which some believe to be attached to being compulsorily detained under the Mental Health Act. On the other hand, the Mental Health Act provides a more rigorous framework for the protection of detained young people.

The review advised that:

> *"In the short-term the unit should develop its own policy on the consideration that it should apply to the use of the legal powers under which children and young persons are admitted. However, local practice illustrates issues of national concern. As any policy will not relate solely to one unit it is recommended that consideration be given to these issues by the Department of Health, the Mental Health Act Commission and other bodies with a view to the Department of Health issuing national guidance".*

At the time of writing this report, no guidance on this matter had been issued by the Department of Health.

The Commission is pleased to note that, as a result of the review, an additional £1.5 million has become available for redevelopment of the unit. In addition, funding has been approved for the appointment of a second consultant psychiatrist and a more senior clinical psychologist. The aim is to develop the treatment activities of the unit to accompany its more traditional assessment role, an initiative which is welcomed by the Commission.

Consent to Treatment

The subject of the consent to treatment of minors is very complex and has been the subject of a number of legal judgements **(Gillick v West Norfolk and Wisbech Area Health Authority (1986), Re W (A Minor) (1992), Re H W and H (Minors) 1983, South Glamorgan County Council v W and B (1993)).**

The Commission is aware that, in relation to this problem the Code of Practice, Chapter 30, is in need of some revision and appropriate suggestions will be put to the Secretary of State in line with the Commission's responsibilities in this matter.

7.2   The Category of "Personality Disorder"

The topic is discussed in Chapter 7.4 in relation to mentally disordered offenders and is highlighted here only to emphasise that the disorder, and the difficulty in treating it, is not peculiar to the offender group of patients.

7.3   Services For Patients With Learning Disability

Treatment and Care of Patients with Learning Disabilities who are unable to make their own Decisions

The treatment and care of people with learning disability who are in-patients in long stay hospitals usually takes place outside the Mental Health Act.

The Commission is aware that a substantial number of people with learning disability rcmain in hospital. This is despite a planned hospital closure programme and the resettlement of numbers of people with learning disability in the community. The number of people with learning disability living in long stay hospitals is between 11,000 and 17,000 in England and Wales. Many of these people lack capacity to consent to treatment or to make a number of other decisions including whether to participate in proposed resettlement plans. The majority of these patients are in hospital "informally", that is, not under a Section of the Mental Health Act. The Code of Practice at paragraph 18.27 gives guidance on the safety of "informal patients" who would be at risk and may require locked doors or close surveillance by nursing staff. The Code recommends that patients who persistently and purposely attempt to leave a ward or nursing home, whether or not they understand the risk, must be considered for a Mental Health Act assessment with a view to a formal detention being implemented. There are many patients in hospital with learning disabilities who cannot make decisions for themselves or provide adequate self care. Many of these patients are living in conditions of security (locked doors) although they are not detained under a section of the Mental Health Act.

The Mental Health Act provides safeguards, particularly with regard to medical treatment (Second Opinion procedure, Part IV of the Mental Health Act), access to the Mental Health Act Commission and a right to apply or be referred to a Mental Health Review Tribunal. The Mental Health Act also gives patients an entitlement to aftercare under Section 117 of the Mental Health Act.

The Commission is concerned that clinical teams should follow the Code of Practice advice on the circumstances under which formal detention should be considered. It is, for example, particularly important that formal detention should be considered for patients receiving high doses of medication who do not have the capacity to understand or consent to their treatment.

It is not acceptable that patients are nursed behind locked doors as a substitute for close nursing supervision and the Commission recommends that a 'locked door' policy be in place to guide implementation and monitoring of the locking of doors and that all treatment decisions be made in the context of a treatment plan which is regularly updated. The Code of Practice makes detailed recommendations about this at paragraph 18.28.

The Commission is aware that this is a time of massive change in the delivery of services for people with learning disability. The Commission has seen many examples of good practice and resettlement programmes incorporating the recommendations of the Mansell Report, the provision of advocacy and detailed care planning in consultation with carers, advocacy groups, purchasers and local voluntary groups.

> ### *Bromham Hospital, South Bedfordshire*
>
> *Members of the Commission who visited observed a resettlement programme which had been carefully planned with all relevant groups and the purchasers to provide a secure facility for six people with learning disability in a community setting. This provision met all the requirements of the Mansell recommendations in providing a local, high quality, individualised service for people with learning disabilities who have behaviour difficulties in conditions of minimum security. This is particularly impressive because it is a non-hospital based provision. Members of the Commission have also noted the high quality of service provided at the Slade Hospital in Oxford for only five patients remaining in hospital: many others are being rehabilitated at long stay hospitals with a view to future resettlement in the community. The service also provides two beds to be used in crisis situations for people with learning disability on site.*

Extension of the Mental Health Act Commission Remit

The Commission has repeatedly requested the Secretary of State that its remit be extended to include patients who are "involuntarily in hospital" but not formally detained. This group includes people referred to above with learning disability who are unable to give informed consent to hospital admission or to continuing stay in hospital and/or a treatment programme. Of particular concern are treatment programmes which include behaviour modification or long term and/or high doses of medication. This group of patients might be described as "de facto" detained and have no external safeguards to protect their rights and monitor care. The Commission continues to request the Secretary of State to extend its jurisdiction to include this group of patients.

Mansell Report

The task of the group preparing this report was to analyse how four successful Community Care services for people with learning disability have approached their task and to synthesise the findings into practical guidance which other local services might consult. The Commission is concerned that the recommendations of the Mansell Report are disseminated as widely as possible to enable purchasers and providers to create an appropriate service for people with learning disability who require some secure care.

> *The Commission is aware that some patients remain in hospital without positive planning to make discharge in the community a possibility. The Commission has information of one patient who was detained on Section 3 for four years with no clear aftercare plan to enable active discharge planning to be made. On three occasions a Mental Health Review Tribunal was unable to discharge this patient because of the inadequate and inappropriate provision in the community. This patient's family requested and finally obtained a Community Care assessment under the provisions of Section 47 of the Community Care Act 1990. As a result of this request a comprehensive assessment was finally completed and a care plan written to enable this patient to be cared for at home rather than in hospital.*

Provision of Information

The Commission considers that information for patients with learning disability about their rights under the Mental Health Act should be provided in a way which can be easily understood and that is readily accessible to them.

Quality of Care

The Commission has observed a general improvement in the quality of the hospital environment for people with a learning disability. Members of the Commission are particularly impressed with the reprovision of services for people with learning disability at Harperbury Hospital in Hertfordshire. The reprovision is in good quality buildings about which all patients commented very positively. The Commission is concerned to note some provision which has been created in old hospital sites which appears to be still bleak and unwelcoming and an example is given below.

> **Penrose House, St Bernard's Hospital at the West London Healthcare NHS Trust:** *new provision*
>
> *Members of the Commission understand that Penrose House was opened as a facility for patients with learning disability in June 1994 and when they visited on 19 January 1995 they found that the front door was locked because one patient was attempting to leave but there was no locked ward policy to guide practice. There were many locked doors within the facility which felt very much like a traditional ward with a bleak general atmosphere. Members of the Commission were told that the last meal of the day was a little after 5 pm and at the time of the visit no occupational therapy input was provided and the input from psychology was recent. The nursing staff whom members of the Commission met had little awareness of the Code of Practice and no copy could be found in the ward. There was little evidence of aftercare planning in the case of a detained patient whose notes were examined. Members of the Commission were disappointed to encounter such relatively poor quality of care, with institutional qualities and a requirement for further training of staff, in a unit set in a large hospital environment, yet opened only recently.*

Patients with Learning Disability in Special Hospitals

This topic is considered in Chapter 9.8

Learning Disabled Patients with Personality Disorders

During the last two years the Commission's attention has been drawn to the extreme difficulties in finding suitable placements for those persons with learning difficulties accompanied by personality disorders who are not easily accommodated in health or social services settings. They are likely to be rejected by health services on the grounds of their anti-social and dangerous behaviours. They are often rejected from social services settings because of their perceived mental health problems.

A small number end up by default in the criminal justice system and within prison settings where prison medical officers have sought advice from the Commission on how to place them in a more appropriate health care setting. Such persons are charged with criminal offences, typically assault, arson or sexual offences against children. They usually have multiple disabilities, including epilepsy. It appears that the very tight definitions in Section 1 of the Mental Health Act are being used to preclude such persons from health care under the provisions of the Act. The Commission is concerned that many Trusts no longer have a facility for helping such people. In 1995 the Commission has become aware that through Home Office direction using Section 48, such persons are beginning to be seen in Regional Secure Units. Medium Secure Units are not properly designed for the care and treatment of such disability. Placement out of Medium Secure Units is proving to be extremely difficult and complicated by ownership and finance for long-term care.

7.4   Services for Difficult and Offender Patients

After accepting the broad principles set out in 1993 in "Report of the Department of Health and Home Office: Review of services for mentally disordered offenders and others requiring similar services", the Government set up, for an initial period of three years, a new committee, again chaired by Dr John Reed, *"To advise the Department of Health and the Home Office on matters referred to it in connection with the provision and co-ordination of services for mentally disordered offenders and others requiring similar services, and to provide advice to the two departments on related issues which are referred to it."* Services for mentally disordered offenders were declared a first order NHS priority for 1994/95.

The result has been to give mentally disordered offenders a high profile and to encourage the publication of guidance for persons working in the services affected. For example, a sequel to the Home Office Circular 66/90 has now been published and The Nuffield Institute has published a helpful Guide to the Mental Health Act for the use of the courts. The National Association for the Care and Rehabilitation of Offenders has prepared a Social Services training package and the Central Council on Education and Social Work has produced specifications for Forensic Social Work which sets out the levels of competence required for persons training in this speciality. This pack was commissioned by the Department of Health. It was issued to the probation services and is being used by some Trusts. The Mental Health Foundation has hosted a series of conferences on the needs of mentally disordered offenders and the topic has been put on the agenda of Area Criminal Justice Liaison Committees. New posts in forensic psychiatry include a Chair in Special Hospital Psychiatry at Broadmoor. Numerous initiatives, particularly in the field of diversion from penal to health services, have started and a variety of research initiatives are being funded by the Home Office and Department of Health of which the Dorset project on the needs of females is just one example.

The impact on local operational practice, however, has been somewhat patchy. Mentally disordered offenders receive little or no mention in many aftercare policy documents. Inter-agency collaboration often proves difficult and there is a clear need for the promotion of good working relationships across the boundaries of the services responsible for assessment and management, including health, personal social services, probation, courts, police, prisons, housing, social security and voluntary organisations. Discrepancies in practice, conflicting responsibilities, complex funding arrangements and issues of confidentiality and communication all have to be overcome. The seriousness of these problems is well illustrated in the series of recent public inquiries into deaths caused by mental patients.

Provision for Difficult to Manage Patients

The report of the Department of Health Working Group on secure provision, published in August 1994, recommended that high security services should be more widely dispersed and cater for no more than 200 patients each. So long as units are of sufficient size to meet the needs of a mixed clientele and to provide the ancillary services presently available in large Special Hospitals, the Commission supports this proposal and hopes that Governmental deliberations will conclude in favour. The Commission welcomes the setting up of the national High Security Commissioning Board as from April 1996 (Chapter 9.8).

The Commission supports strongly the Working Group's recommendation that NHS commissioning contracts should aim to meet the needs of patients, including those with learning disabilities, who may have a longer-term need for medium security and, following discharge, may require hostel accommodation with 24 hour cover. Given the frequent use of the independent sector to relieve pressure on beds for difficult patients, commissioning agencies need to include appropriate requirements for aftercare in contracts to ensure that, notwithstanding difficulties in liaison between independent hospitals and a variety of distant social services, government guidelines on discharge are closely followed in these cases. There are particular problems in implementation of Supervision Register requirements for patients hospitalised far from home.

There was an allocation of £45 million from central funds for medium secure services between 1991-5, with further contributions from regional budgets: an additional £4.4 million revenue funding for places was announced in September 1994. The Glancy Report's recommended target of 1,000 medium secure beds has been met, but this is less than the target of 2,000 beds proposed by the Butler Report over twenty years ago.

Pressure on beds for difficult to manage patients is frequently drawn to the attention of members of the Commission. Scarcity of provision outside of forensic units causes a 'silting up' of facilities that were meant only for short term or acute needs. This impedes essential exchanges between facilities and delays therapeutic progressions through different levels of security. The development of diversion schemes has also increased demand. Long waits for admission or transfer persist and some of the difficulties experienced by the Courts in accessing beds has attracted adverse publicity. At present, most Regional Secure Units operate a policy whereby only persons charged with serious offences are admitted. The units' function as assessment centres for patients requiring security during a remand for reports is being adversely affected by the need to provide for an increased number of transfers from prison of sentenced offenders.

Many of the less serious and less acutely disturbed patients could be assessed and treated outside the specialist forensic services. This is not always possible due to the difficulties for hard-pressed local psychiatrists in finding sufficient time required for patients involved in court proceedings. This often includes consultation and negotiation with nursing and other staff prior to an agreement to accept an offender. The scarcity of locked facilities and facilities for long term treatment of patients requiring a degree of security discourages general psychiatrists who might otherwise be able to relieve some of the pressure.

The Commission would have liked to have seen more detailed consideration given in the discussion of secure provision to the problems faced by women. These differ both in scale and in kind from those of male offender patients. In particular, the danger to others is not so great, although self harm is more prevalent, and appropriate security can often be achieved by improved staffing rather than by physical barriers. The disproportionate number of males among patients needing high or medium security means that women may suffer from attempts to integrate the sexes. In Medium Secure Units one or two women are sometimes placed in an otherwise all male population that includes known sexual predators. Women patients need regimes and activities suited to their needs and benefit from female contacts and supports.

Psychopathic Disorder

The report of the Working Group on psychopathic disorders was preceded by the publication of a review of treatment and research issues by Bridget Dolan and Jeremy Coid. After an exhaustive search through the literature they found the available evidence insufficient to demonstrate the efficacy of any specific treatment method and pointed to the need for more exact diagnostic work and improved treatment evaluation. Given this uncertainty, it is unsurprising that the Working Group did not produce a blueprint for a radically new service.

Many psychiatrists are sceptical of the ability to treat of psychopaths by available medical methods. Clinicians in the Special Hospitals have long been concerned that some individuals with this diagnosis committed by the courts on Section 41 Restriction Orders prove unamenable or resistive to therapy and sometimes disruptive to the treatment of others; yet they must be kept indefinitely occupying a hospital place. The Working Group proposed the introduction of a 'hybrid' order, permitting the courts to couple a hospital committal with a notional prison sentence to come into force if treatment fails. The Commission does not support this suggestion. A continuing threat of transfer to prison under the 'hybrid' order could be anti-therapeutic, could sour relations between patients and staff; or it might enable patients to avoid confronting their problems by engineering a retreat to prison. Instead, trial periods in hospital could be arranged by making better use of interim hospital orders under Section 38 or on remands to hospital for reports under Section 35 and 36. The Working Party proposes an extension of interim hospital orders from six to twelve months. In our Fifth Biennial Report (p. 43) the Commission queried the restriction of Section 36 to a time limit of twelve weeks. More frequent use of Restriction Orders with a set limit of time would reduce the prospect of interminable hospitalisations.

Recognising the problems of providing for the many varieties and degrees of personality disorder encountered among discharged prisoners as well as among clients of the psychiatric services, the Commission supports the Working Party's proposals to set up a joint Health and Home Office programme of research in which specific treatments would be applied to carefully defined problems and the outcomes evaluated over long periods. The Commission considers, however, that the enterprise should have adequate central funding and be nationally co-ordinated. Small local initiatives are unlikely to yield definitive results. In the light of the admitted inadequacy of present provision for these difficult clients the Commission supports very strongly the proposal for more specialist units, such as the Henderson Hospital. All these proposals have serious resource implications which are not squarely faced in the report of the Working Party.

Supervision Register

The setting up of Supervision Registers of patients at risk to themselves or others raises particular issues in relation to mentally disordered offenders. Some health units are interpreting the directives as indicating that all patients committed by the courts, transferred from prison or on Section 41 Restriction Orders should go on the register automatically. The Commission is concerned that the fact of having been on a Section of the Mental Health Act should not, in itself, be regarded as reason enough for inclusion. Placement of too many persons on the register risks diverting scarce resources to the possible detriment of others. There is further discussion of the Supervision Register in Chapter 10.3.

Persons living in the community and presenting themselves voluntarily to forensic psychiatric services may be discouraged from initiating or continuing contact if they fear their names may appear on a register. Their anxiety about potential breaches of confidentiality and the imposition of a stigmatising label are not entirely irrational.

Difficult-to-manage patients and those with a history of offending are not welcomed by clinicians who feel they lack the facilities to cope with them. The new Registers may therefore possibly produce further resistance to the admission to hospital of individuals with manifest behavioural problems. The result could be that some very difficult cases are left to be dealt with by the already over-burdened community services.

If the Register is to be of practical value it must be restricted to cases of special need. The Commission looks forward to the evaluation of the impact of Supervision Registers.

Diversion from the Criminal Justice System

The inappropriate processing of mentally disordered individuals through the criminal justice system is a long-standing problem. The Commission welcomes Home Office initiatives in publicising avenues for diversion and funding court diversion schemes: over 100 such schemes are now operating.

The policy of diversion, however, needs to be accompanied by a corresponding increase in mental health resources. There is no doubt that in the central areas of large conurbations, where demand is high and facilities are already under strain, diversion increases the pressure on mental health services. The Commission is concerned there should be adequate facilities for those 'diverted' which do not compete unfairly with the needs of others. Moreover, there are marginal cases, both among persistent minor offenders and some who commit grave offences, where it is questionable whether non-prosecution is in the best interests of either the offender or society. A Crown Prosecution Service decision not to prosecute serious assaults or offences such as arson, because the offender is already in contact with a psychiatric service, can lessen a patient's chances of access to long-term control and supervision

Since mentally disordered offenders form such a small proportion of the clients of the police and the courts, it may be impracticable to set up specialised diversionary schemes everywhere, but some form of co-ordination is generally needed. Court Liaison Schemes to provide swift mental health assessments on the spot have proliferated and have certainly reduced the number of remands to prison for psychiatric assessment in areas where they operate effectively [11] but by no means all courts have access to them and few of the formal projects maintain a presence at court five days a week. Most schemes allow for the attendance one day a week of a community psychiatric nurse and a psychiatrist, but this still involves some remands in custody pending assessment. The prevention of delay and unnecessary remands to prison depends on the availability of a psychiatrist with access to hospital places. At present many schemes are still developing and are dependent on temporary pump-priming funding or on individuals whose commitment may not be permanent. There is as yet no national standard of service. Thus an offender's chances of diversion can depend very largely on whether the court hearing the case has an established system or well developed contacts with local services. So far the national impact of these schemes, as measured by numbers of immediate committals to hospital or remands to hospital for assessment, does not appear very great.

Assessment with a view to early admission to hospital on a Section of the Mental Health Act for offenders who are actively psychotic covers only a small minority of offenders with mental health needs. Many are mentally ill without being sectionable or needing urgent admission to hard pressed acute beds. Many have problems of personality disorder, alcohol and drug abuse, sexual deviance or learning disability and often acute housing or financial problems aggravate their condition. They concern the Commission because, left without help, they may become sectionable. In some areas they are dealt with by panel assessment schemes [12] run by professional representatives from probation, social services, mental health and sometimes housing. In suitable cases, a package of care can be offered to the courts, perhaps including a temporary stay in hospital, which avoids unnecessary penal custody. Such schemes are dependent on active inter-agency co-operation. They require commitment from higher management, formal recognition of responsibilities, necessary funding allocations and access to hostels for offenders who are homeless or cannot be left in ordinary accommodation. Panel assessment procedures, even more than the medically oriented court psychiatry liaison schemes, are hampered by the limited resources available in some areas.

Remands To Prison And Transfers From Prison

The Commission continues to be concerned at the disproportionate number of remands to prison for the purpose of obtaining psychiatric reports. It is evident that the legal provision for remands for this purpose to hospital under Section 35 remains under used and that bail hostels prepared to admit the mentally disordered are scarce. The numerous but scattered court diversion schemes have so far failed to remedy the situation.

Transfers to hospital of both sentenced and remand prisoners have substantially increased, but the average waiting time for hospital placements is still too long. The process of identifying the area responsible and finding an amenable facility can cause long delay in the transfer of sentenced prisoners and even when Hospital Orders are completed they are often implemented very close to the 28 day legal limit.

A pilot scheme for a psychiatric service to prisoners on remand is in operation at the Bentham Unit of the West London Healthcare NHS Trust. The project depends on temporary central funding, so its future is uncertain. It functions in a locked ward in a renovated block of the old St Bernard's Hospital, Ealing and takes male patients from the former North West Thames RHA region who are in prison on remand. Medical and nursing staff visit the prisons regularly to carry out assessments at the request of prison medical officers. For those patients considered in need and suitable for admission they are able to arrange swift Home Office authorisation for immediate transfer under Section 48. Although effective in promoting and accelerating transfers, the project has encountered problems. The unit cannot accept patients requiring very high security. Those selected may not always be patients considered by the prison medical staff to be the most needy in terms of behavioural disturbance. Prisoners from outside the defined catchment area are necessarily excluded from consideration.

Finding placements for patients when the court proceedings are completed can sometimes be difficult. A patient who is acquitted may still need treatment, as in the case of Christopher Clunis. Many receive hospital orders, but have to wait up to 28 days for a place in the admitting hospital. To avoid a return to prison during this wait the unit has allowed men to return to the ward as a place of safety but apparently, they are entitled to refuse treatment, until they are transferred from there.

The worst delays and disruptions to smooth clinical progress are occasioned by legal procedures. Magistrates often remand repeatedly for short periods and require prisoners to be present each time even when they are in hospital. This makes heavy demands on staff and can be stressful for patients. The unit accepts patients from the area who are remanded to hospital on Section 35 or 36 via court diversion schemes. Section 35 gives no power to treat without consent. When magistrates refer to Crown Court patients who have been on this section, they fall into legal limbo and, in the absence of a Section 48 transfer warrant from the Home Office, must return to prison. Virtually all transfers from prison on Section 48 have restriction orders attached. The Home Office is reluctant to agree to onward transfer of restricted patients to more appropriate hospital accommodation before their court cases have been finally settled. In the case of Crown Court hearings this may not be for many months, with the result that beds become blocked, which adds to the cost of the service and creates anxiety and uncertainty for patients and staff.

Any system of transfer on remand is hampered by the limited applicability of Section 48, which refers to "urgent need" (although that phrase is often interpreted liberally) and excludes psychopaths and all but the "severely" mentally impaired. The Working Group on psychopathic disorders has argued that they should not be excluded and the necessity for the other restrictions could also be questioned.

While welcoming the aim of swift transfer of remand prisoners, the Commission is aware of these legal and administrative barriers and recognises the desirability of providing a nation-wide service rather than a local experiment. The heavy demand for such a service suggests that too many potential patients are being remanded in custody in the first place. Diversion is most satisfactory the earlier in the process it can be accomplished, preferably soon after arrest and before prosecution.

In those instances where hospital treatment leads to recovery before the date when a transferred prisoner is due for release, there is a requirement to return to prison rather than to have the benefit of release via a mental health aftercare plan. The risk of relapse may be increased by this arbitrary procedure.

Mentally Disordered Offenders and the Payment of Welfare Benefits

The Commission has been aware for some time of the disparity in eligibility for the Disability Living Allowance between different categories of detained patients in the Special Hospitals, RSUs, Registered Mental Nursing Homes and other units. Under an amendment (1992 13) to Social Security Regulations, someone who is serving a prison sentence and is then transferred to hospital as a restricted patient under Section 47/49 of the Mental Health Act is disqualified from receiving the Disability Living Allowance (DLA). These patients are deemed to be prisoners for as long as a direction restricting their discharge is in force or until the date on which they would have expected to have been released had they not been so transferred.

In effect, this means that there are patients, whose severity of mental impairment would entitle them to the mobility component of the DLA, who are disqualified from receiving it, while others in the same unit with a similar degree of impairment receive the benefit by virtue of the fact that they were transferred to hospital via a court rather than a prison. The Commission considers that these regulations give rise to inequities in the entitlements of similar groups of patients. The considerable disparities in income which result are also sometimes a source of difficulty in the units where they occur. The Commission recommends that the regulations are reconsidered.

The Commission has also recently had brought to its attention the fact that there are still fairly widespread misunderstandings about these complex regulations both in the Benefits Agency itself and among patients and their advisers, with the result that mistakes are being made and some patients on Section 37/41 are being debarred from the DLA in error. The Commission hopes that the Benefits Agency will consider issuing clear guidance on these matters for its officers and customers alike. (There is further discussion of welfare benefits in Chapter 10.9).

Police Diversion Via Section 136

A constable's power to convey from a public place to a place of safety for assessment a person who appears mentally disordered can avoid the unnecessary charging and processing through the penal system of individuals who commit minor offences of public disorder as a result of their apparent illness. Continuing evidence of the uneven and differing use of this section is apparent to members of the Commission in the course of their visits.

Police authorities still operate differing policies, there is no national monitoring and central statistics of usage are not available, although practice in this area appears to be improving. Some police stations can supply statistics only after laborious searching through custody records. In some areas, where information is not systematically recorded, members of the Commission have been told that the legal status of prospective patients brought to hospital by the police is not always clear. Department of Health statistics of Section 136 procedures and documentation should be standardised. The Commission is aware that the

Department of Health and the Home Office are currently considering this issue. The Commission is seeking to build up a more accurate picture of the use of Section 136 through inquiry to Social Services who are responsible for providing the assessments by Approved Social Workers. In December 1994 the Metropolitan Police (who already make use of a convenient form for recording reasons when the section is invoked) instituted a training scheme for police dealing with mental disorder. In collaboration with the National Schizophrenia Fellowship they have produced a helpful training video.

There are differences of view about the use of police stations rather than hospitals as places of safety. Assessment at a police station can often involve detention in a cell, exposure to an intimidating environment, and contact with arrested persons. Many Trusts, pleading lack of space or funding and concerns about security, remain reluctant to provide accommodation. However, where facilities have been provided, the system seems to operate smoothly without creating the difficulties anticipated, as for example at St. Anne's Hospital in Poole, Dorset. The Commission recommends that, ordinarily, the place of safety should be a hospital in preference to a police station.

Completing multi-disciplinary Section 136 assessments swiftly is the first priority. Delays due to difficulty in obtaining Section 12 approved doctors or in securing an ASW from a limited out-of-hours team are still being experienced, as are further delays if there is no available bed in the relevant catchment area hospital. In some areas, where hospitals are used as places of safety, constables are required to check with custody officers before using Section 136, but it is illegal to move the subject from one place of safety to another once assessment has been instigated. The role and training of forensic medical examiners, a topic raised in the report of the Royal Commission on the Criminal Justice System, is also a matter of some concern. Notwithstanding many continuing problems, an increasing number of areas now have detailed Section 136 policies jointly agreed between health, social services and police, with recording systems and liaison committees to monitor the operation. An Avon and Somerset working party have produced detailed policy guidelines on Section 136 procedures and on more general provisions for mentally disordered persons in police custody. The existing model schemes in Hampshire and in Devon and Cornwall, which also involved the Crown Prosecution Service, are reported to have been successful and effective.

Determining Responsibility for Patient Care

Social, health and judicial services have boundaries that are not necessarily coterminous. A person may appear in a court in one location but be under probation, health and social services each from a different geographical division. The internal market demands specific ownership and sorting this out can take a long time, particularly when one agency refuses to accept responsibility. Notwithstanding detailed instructions from the Department of Health, it can take months to settle such issues, leaving patients languishing in prison or occupying hospital places unnecessarily.

Under the rules of the internal market a person who commits an offence far from home and is arraigned at a distant court remains the responsibility of the psychiatric service in his home area. That service may reasonably decline to take responsibility at the behest of a distant court liaison psychiatrist without first examining the patient but the time or funding to do this may not be available. If the matter is not settled after repeated remands, the court may impose a prison sentence *faute de mieux.*

Decisions to admit patients from prisons are not entirely the responsibility of the psychiatrist. Permission often has to be sought from the purchasers for extra-contractual referrals. Arrangements may be further complicated when the prison service moves remand prisoners around the country.

The prison service is now a purchaser of NHS services, but prison medical officers may have difficulty in establishing contact with psychiatric services prepared to assess and arrange transfer of mentally ill prisoners. The problem is aggravated by the fact that so many prisoners are housed far from the service that officially 'owns' them. Delivery of good quality psychiatric care to patients remaining in prison is further hampered by the structure of the prison day and the difficulty of access to multi-disciplinary teams.

Occupational Therapy for Mentally Disordered Offenders

Individuals who are both patients and criminals have multiple and complex problems, often very chronic, which have implications for attempts at social and family reintegration and the possibility of employment. Recognising these particular needs, the College of Occupational Therapists has set up a special interest group on work in secure facilities where there is a diversity of patients, many with serious skills deficits or showing the effects of institutionalisation, some of whom require intensive and prolonged rehabilitation. Recreational activities to combat the boredom and restricted leisure facilities associated with confinement are important, but close observation and assessment of each patient is essential, leading to well-planned individualised programmes and the setting of realistic goals. Professional skills are needed for the management in a controlled, measurable way of specific risks, such as the gradual introduction of tools to patients with low frustration tolerance or inability to function in group situations.

Whilst there is a national shortage of qualified, state registered occupational therapists, most forensic psychiatric services have recognised and addressed the need for occupational therapy input by establishing posts in all areas, from prisons to interim secure units. Even though many such posts remain vacant their importance is acknowledged. The unique contribution occupational therapy can make to the assessment and treatment of people who have multiple and complex problems spanning social, educational, functional, economic and cultural difficulties is integral to a complete treatment programme. The dual stigma of having a psychiatric and criminal record has major implications for the future employment prospects of many service users and is addressed by occupational therapists by setting graded, achievable goals.

A special interest group of occupational therapists working in secure environments is well established and meets regularly to address the problems of providing a comprehensive assessment and treatment service for a diverse group of patients ranging from short stay patients being assessed prior to court appearance through to long term, slow stream patients requiring intensive rehabilitation to address serious skills defects and institutionalisation.

It is important to differentiate between the undeniable need for the provision of recreational activities to combat the boredom associated with confinement and lack of access to leisure facilities and the need for systematic assessment and carefully tailored rehabilitation programmes which facilitate the acquisition of skills necessary for independent living.

The assessment of dangerousness and predictability is part of every occupational therapy activity and is carried out by gradually introducing specific risk elements into the treatment programme in a controlled, systematic and measurable way. This may involve use of tools and implements or it may mean careful observation and assessment of a person's frustration tolerance in particular circumstances or attitude towards authority and ability to empathise in a group setting.

Urgent Notification from the Home Office: Leave for Restricted Patients

On the 5th December 1994 the Home Office announced the Secretary of State's decision that, subject to such exception as he might consider appropriate in the circumstance of any particular case, he would normally no longer give his consent for restricted patients to have escorted or unescorted leave of absence from hospital for holidays or holiday-type activity. This decision was conveyed to all RMOs and was to be effected immediately.

The Commission was assured by the Home Office that applications for leave would still be considered as they had been previously, but in addition applications would need the personal approval of the Home Secretary. The new arrangements have had the effect of limiting leave arrangements in some cases, but mostly applications appear to have been dealt with fairly and sympathetically and the decisions have been made promptly.

Aftercare

Notwithstanding the long-established statutory requirement of Section 117 and the more recently established Care Programme Approach, the task of arranging adequate aftercare for forensic patients is often difficult. Scarcity of appropriately staffed hostels or other accommodation delays discharges. Purchasers need to become more involved in checking when realistic care programmes for difficult patients cannot be implemented within the resources provided.

A series of disasters leading to official inquiries have highlighted these problems. It is right that such circumstances should be publicised, but disproportionate media attention to the dangerousness of a few patients can make acceptance of mentally disordered offenders in community placements more difficult.

Patients presenting intermittent mental illness with an underlying anti-social personality disorder often fare badly under existing arrangements. Acute psychiatric services aim to bring psychotic symptoms under control as swiftly as possible, usually by means of medication. Few health facilities, however, are geared to long-term control of challenging behaviour arising from personality disorder, so there is a tendency to discharge such patients to inadequate aftercare provision as soon as their psychotic phase subsides. This happened in the case of Michael Buchanan about which an independent inquiry was ordered (North West London Mental Health NHS Trust, 1994). This patient had a lifelong history of criminal offending, much of it linked to drug abuse. He was admitted to mental hospital for the thirteenth time, but was discharged from his Section 37 hospital order within a month once his acute psychosis had subsided. Some two weeks later he robbed and killed an old man and was convicted of manslaughter by virtue of diminished responsibility. In spite of evidence that he had been suffering from paranoid schizophrenia the Special Hospitals Service Authority would not accept him and he was sentenced to life imprisonment. The Commission would endorse one of the recommendations of the inquiry, that the 'availability of medium secure accommodation should be extended' so that such patients could receive longer term treatment.

The media rightly give publicity to inquiries into disastrous incidents involving patients on aftercare, but the Commission shares the concern of the Royal College of Psychiatrists that an exaggerated reputation for violence may be created. The inquiry into the tragedy of Christopher Clunis emphasised that, although some patients present special risks, the public should be made aware that most mentally disordered individuals can live quite safely in the community, that when they do commit offences as a result of illness these are usually minor and that serious violence is a rarity.

7.5 Elderly Mentally Ill

The Commission's Fifth Biennial Report reported that the Commission is frequently asked to comment on whether elderly patients with dementia or other organic brain syndromes which impair their mental capacity to make reasoned judgements should be detained for care and treatment under the provisions of the Act or can be admitted and cared for informally. The Commission's Chief Executive visited Cornwall mental health services to discuss this issue because of the increased use of the Act for such patients.

The Commission considers that each case must be considered on its merits. The majority of older people with dementia are willing to accept the care and treatment offered to them and can be admitted as informal patients.

Where the patient actively refuses treatment, the Commission recommends that an assessment for treatment under the Mental Health Act is undertaken. Many of the patients who persistently wander away from the ward or actively resist treatment, including medication or nursing care, are "de facto" detained, when they might properly be detained under the Act. The Act provides a surer legal framework for staff to make decisions and affords an opportunity for such a patient's detention to be reviewed by the Managers and Mental Health Review Tribunals at regular intervals.

Another issue often raised in connection with elderly, confused patients is the covert administration of medication. This topic is considered in Chapter 5. Other legal aspects of the treatment of incapable patients are covered in Chapter 2.

8 *Special Issues*

8.1   Definition and Availability of Section 12 Doctors

Section 12 (2) of the 1983 Act stipulates that one of the medical recommendations for the purpose of an application under the Act "shall be given by a practitioner approved by the Secretary of State as having special experience in the diagnosis or treatment of mental disorder" and is not to be confused, as sometimes happens, with the second medical recommendation, which "shall, if practicable, be given by a registered medical practitioner who has such previous acquaintance (with the patient)". When a such a doctor is not available then "it is desirable for the second medical recommendation to be given by an 'approved' doctor" (Code of Practice 12.25).

The Act itself under Section 12(3-6) gives further guidance on the suitability of doctors to give the second medical recommendation.

The Code of Practice (12.38) suggests that Health Authorities and Trusts should take action to increase the number of Section 12 doctors by including within their job descriptions a service obligation to become approved.

Two problems have been frequently reported to the Commission:

- It is often found that a S12 approved doctor cannot be located rapidly when a patient urgently requires an assessment for admission to hospital under the Act. This may be due to an actual shortage of doctors or to the fact that they are unable or are unwilling to be called out, often at night or at the weekend to make a recommendation. In the absence of such a recommendation, the patient may be admitted under an emergency Section 4 or more often is taken to and held in hospital under a doctor's or nurse's holding power, Sections 5(2) or 5(4).

- General Practitioners are increasingly organising themselves into large rotas or co-operatives to provide emergency out-of-hours services. Thus, the doctor who knows the patient may not be available when needed by the duty doctor.

The Department of Health has advised the Commission that:

- The deputising doctor cannot be considered "to have prior knowledge of the patient simply because he has access to the patient's records".

- The GPs deputising/ answering service should contact the actual GP if it appears from the telephone call that a mental health assessment is likely.

A further possibility is for GPs and their deputising services to ensure that a Section 12 approved doctor is available when required.

Commission members visiting hospitals are sometimes told that a few of the Section 12 doctors are not well-informed about their requirements under the Act and that the second medical recommendation from a doctor who knows the patient is often "merely rubber stamping the views of the psychiatrist". The Commission believes that there is a good case for additional training of general practitioners in their responsibilities under the Mental Health Act and in mental health generally and for more rigorous approval procedures for Section 12 doctors.

8.2   Police

The Commission has been pleased to note the considerable improvement in police training and operational policies which followed publication of the Clunis Report.

An example of this is the Metropolitan Police Service where all operational officers up to the rank of Inspector are receiving specialist training in recognising and dealing with mentally disordered people.

A significant development in London has been the appointment, on each Division, of a Mental Health Liaison Officer of supervisory rank with specific responsibilities for liaising with hospitals and other relevant agencies. A useful guide for police officers dealing with people with mental illness has also been produced.

The Commission understands that similar initiatives have been taken up in other police forces and welcomes this enhancement in the police response to dealing with people with mental disorder.

8.3   Ethnic Issues

Introduction

Black and minority ethnic groups continue to experience considerable disadvantages in the provision of mental health services because of the difficulty in obtaining treatment which is appropriate to their need.

Several studies have found that, among patients referred to the psychiatric services, there is a higher rate of schizophrenia in the African-Caribbean population in the UK compared to non- African-Caribbean samples. The reasons for this remain unclear and there is little definitive evidence. Several hypotheses have been advanced, including misdiagnosis, biological differences and differences in the way in which psychiatric services are accessed.

However, it is clear that the black population generally perceives the psychiatric services on offer as being unwelcome, unsupportive and alien to their culture and needs. The higher admission rates for schizophrenia in this group may possibly reflect the fact that black people usually come for help from the services at a time when they are in crisis, having received little or no help from primary care services, outpatient services or community mental health teams.

The Commission considers that there is a need for research effected with support and commitment from the African-Caribbean community and relevant mental health organisations. In addition, there is a need for statutory organisations to harmonise their efforts in scrutinising services, evaluating existing data and generating further research to examine the issues from a multi-agency perspective. There should be an alliance formed with the African-Caribbean community to support basic research, while ensuring that services continue to develop in a manner which will improve their accessibility and acceptability to the black population.

Since many black patients live in the main urban areas, the general problem of overcrowding in urban acute psychiatric facilities often leads to the admission of black patients who require care under detention to Registered Mental Nursing Homes far from their home area, friends and family (Chapter 9.7). Consequently it is not unusual for patients from these communities to feel isolated, misunderstood, and discriminated against.

The Mental Health Task Force, after consulting service users, concluded that there is a need to make services "more responsive to the needs of people from different ethnic and cultural backgrounds, ensuring that representatives of local communities are involved in service planning and development".

The Commission's concerns about mental health provision for black people continue to centre on matters which have been commented on in the previous five Biennial Reports of the Commission, that is;

- there are disproportionate numbers of patients of Afro-Caribbean origin detained under the Mental Health Act

- many Health Authorities do not address the needs of ethnic minority groups and

- ethnic monitoring (mandatory since 1 April 1995) is still implemented patchily. Many purchasers do not appear to include a requirement for ethnic monitoring in contracts.

Despite Department of Health initiatives in several areas the Commission considers that there has not been as much progress made 'on the ground' in acknowledging and addressing the issues mentioned above as it would have wished. However, it is aware of some initiatives which demonstrate that some general progress is being made. Increasingly, Commissioners find examples where links are being forged between hospitals and local ethnic minority community services.

Many Trusts have taken measures to improve the variety of food available to patients to suit the ethnic mix of their patients, although often it is very badly cooked because of lack of expertise. Several have identified interpreter services, although many of these are inadequate and inappropriate because the interpreters are not trained in mental health work. Some Trusts have used social workers from ethnic minority backgrounds as interpreters, but this has caused concern to the social workers involved because of a possible conflict of interest.

The availability of rights leaflets in languages other than English appears to be patchy even in units with relatively high numbers of patients whose first language is not English.

Ethnic Issues in Registered Mental Nursing Homes

The Commission is concerned at the general lack of proper ethnic monitoring of either staff or patients in Registered Mental Nursing Homes. Little racism awareness training appears to have been given to staff. Within the hospitals there is a large number of ethnic minority patients yet there are very few ethnic minority staff. The Commission is aware that Kneesworth House Hospital in particular has made very serious attempts to attract and recruit staff from ethnic minority backgrounds. Their attempts have not been successful largely because of the geographic location of the hospital.

Ethnic Issues in Special Hospitals

Approximately 19 percent of patients in the Special Hospitals come from black and other ethnic minority communities. The SHSA inquiry into the death of Orville Blackwood (SHSA 1983), referred to in the Fifth Biennial Report, addressed the issues of racism at Broadmoor Hospital and determined that whilst there was no overt racism, there was a more subtle, subconscious and non-deliberate form. It is the Commission's impression that this is generally true at all three Special Hospitals but there has been an encouraging decline in concerns expressed to Commission members by patients about racially prejudiced behaviour.

All three hospitals have established equal opportunities groups and have involved external consultants and patient groups. The Commission welcomes the various cultural events organised to meet the social needs of ethnic minority groups. Continual care will be required to ensure that the needs of minority groups are met, including the provision of high quality ethnic food, special hair care and early access to specialists. Equally important will be the further development of training to enable staff to improve their ability to identify and respond appropriately to the needs of this important group of patients.

Ethnic Issues within the Commission

The Commission is committed to giving proper attention to issues of race and culture within its own organisation.

This has been particularly demonstrated by the recent large scale recruitment exercise of Commission members when job advertisements were placed in black and ethnic minority press. An analysis of the data acquired in the recruitment exercise is given in Chapter 1.2. Race and ethnic issues will also form an important part of the training programme for new members.

The Commission's communication group is addressing how it can improve the quality and accessibility of its communications with ethnic groups including the translation of its information leaflets into ethnic minority languages.

The Commission's Race and Culture Policy is at Appendix 8.3.

8.4 Women's Issues

Over the last two years the Commission has become increasingly concerned about the position of women patients detained in hospital in acute and long-term rehabilitation wards. It is not unusual, for example, to find only two women on a ward where the rest of the patients are men. This often results in experience of an inappropriate male orientated rehabilitation programme. Women in this situation often suffer a lack of privacy and experience some harassment from aggressive male patients. On some acute wards mixed gender sleeping areas often cause unease and concern amongst female patients. This is especially true when doors have no locks, and/or toilet facilities are unisex.

> *In one Commission report to a Medium Secure Unit it is recorded that:*
>
> *"A member of the Community Health Council expressed concern with regard to the possibility of women being at risk on mixed wards. Management gave assurance that every care was taken to ensure the safety of all patients being cared for in the unit. If rape featured in the history of any of the male patients, then extra vigilance was undertaken."*

The Patients Charter specifies that Trusts "must ensure that all patients are told prior to planned admission if they will be in a mixed sex ward". It also specifies that "patients can expect single sex washing and toilet facilities. If you would prefer to be cared for in single sex accommodation (either a single sex ward or bay within a larger ward which offers equal privacy), your wishes will be respected wherever possible". Unlike many other categories of patients, those detained under the Mental Health Act cannot defer their admission to hospital if single sex accommodation is not available and it is therefore even more important that women are given, except in exceptional circumstances, the privacy and dignity of separate facilities which they should expect under the Charter.

The Commission considers that there is a need for greater sensitivity and staff training in relation to women's issues. One of the major needs is to enable women to feel that they have some degree of control over their appearance by being able to choose clothes, having access to cosmetics, and hairdressing facilities.

Women's Issues In Registered Mental Nursing Homes

Women patients are a disadvantaged minority on the wards. The Commission receives many complaints from women patients concerning lack of privacy and harassment by other patients. Separate sleeping areas are not available, though hospital staff do attempt some segregation. Designated male and female toilets and bathrooms are usually provided, though women patients will often complain that their facilities are used by male patients.

Staff sensitivity to women's issues, particularly with regard to sexual harassment, needs encouragement and training. Women patients are encouraged to report instances of concern, but staff responses give patients the impression that these concerns are not given the seriousness and due attention that is required.

Women's Issues in Special Hospitals

Women represent only a small minority (16%) of the patients in the Special Hospitals. Many of them are considered not to require the secure provision of the Special Hospitals but in many instances there are no other suitable facilities to which they could be transferred. In the last two years, considerable effort has been devoted by the SHSA and the Hospitals to identify a strategy for the future provision of services to women in the Special Hospitals, and its publication is imminent. It is clear that this general issue will need to be one of the first to be addressed by the Commissioning Board.

A starting point for any enquiry into women's issues in the Special Hospitals is the Ashworth Hospital Inquiry report which concluded that women patients in Ashworth Hospital have "special difficulties". These difficulties largely stem from their past histories of sexual abuse and male violence. The report concluded that this background was not sufficiently appreciated within the hospital.

Over the last two years, each hospital has identified the women's needs as a discrete service component. They have appointed managers to lead such services and to focus on the problems of women patients. These are important foundations for the further progress which is essential.

At **Ashworth** Hospital all the women's wards, apart from one which is due to transfer in November 1995, are now located on the East site in the "specialist services" clinical area. However, this has raised concerns about the privacy and safety of female patients as there will also be three male wards and one mixed ward within the same area. The argument in favour of such amalgamation is that the female patients, who can be described as "less dangerous", would benefit from a more open site but the lack of funding available to provide a secure perimeter fence has prevented this from happening. The female patients on the mixed ward have only limited access to fresh air, when there are sufficient staff available. On the other wards, the women only have access to a central court and they are currently unable to enjoy any ground parole.

The lack of use of work-areas by women is a continuing problem. Women refuse to go to work activities as they are subject to intimidation both in the mixed-sex transport provided and in the North site, including its mixed-sex recreation areas.

At **Rampton** Hospital, Commission Members have gained the impression, particularly from talking to women patients, that the services available for them are, in important respects, inferior to those offered to men. As a result female patients appear to be marginalised and dis-empowered, to the extent that any therapeutic benefit that could be derived from their stay in hospital is diminished. The culture of Rampton Hospital remains male dominated, and issues specific to their gender are perceived as secondary rather than primary to their care needs.

There are opportunities for female patients to work in the traditional workshops, such as carpentry, printing, weaving, pottery or book binding. At most, some of these activities are attended by only two or three female patients. The minority position of female patients, together with prevalent sexism, often results in female patients leaving their chosen work and preferring to remain on the ward. Motivation of patients to continue work is often non-existent.

There are few specialist services for women. An exception is the Ashby Day Centre, an all female facility which takes self referrals. It consists of 25 places which offer therapy through activity structured to individual needs. Therapeutic counselling services are available for both acute and chronic patients. The therapy offered is part of the patient's treatment plan and is based on the patient's own perceived needs.

The reported benefits of mixed male and female staff on wards appear to favour male patients. Female staff introduce a softening element and allow for the "testing" of male patients who may have sexual problems. The benefits of male staff on female wards are not so clear. Commission members understand that male staff have been offered training about women's issues but few have taken up the offer. Interactions between patients and staff vary in quantity and quality. Use of inappropriate language gives cause for concern and needs to be addressed at staff recruitment, training and appraisal.

Commission members have observed that, in the main, women patients are very poorly dressed. Little effort is made to enhance the patient's individuality or self esteem. Patients appear to accept that their clothes are replaced for them and they retain choice or control over their appearance with difficulty.

At **Broadmoor** Hospital, Commission members have noted that difficulties in recruiting the right gender balance of staff have been reported on the female wards, leading to a preponderance of male staff. Women also appear to be at a disadvantage compared to men in relation to access to fresh air, in that their access to garden areas is even more restricted than that of their male counterparts, as is their access to the canteen. Complaints that they are not allowed, on occasions, to visit the hairdressers are often received from women. Many women appear to be overweight, an issue which the Commission understands is being addressed. Commission members are also concerned at the greater use of seclusion and polypharmacy in relation to women patients. Recent examples of male and female patients having intimate relationships have led to the female ward staff assuming a more restrictive (some might call it protective) stance towards their patients than staff on male wards.

8.5 Health Commissioning & the Mental Health Act Commission

In the Fourth Biennial Report, the emerging importance of Health Commissioning Agencies, consequent upon the implementation of the NHS and Community Care Act 1990 was acknowledged (Chapter 3 - page 16).

In the two years under review, this process has accelerated and the Commission recognises that Health Commissioning Agencies and the manner in which it relates to them are making an increasingly important contribution to the way in which the Commission can pursue its statutory remit. Whilst the focus of Commission visiting activity will always remain provider units, the Commission now ensures that its visit reports are copied to each provider's main Health Commissioner. Increasingly, representatives of Health Commissioning Agencies meet members of the Commission on visits and attend feedback meetings. At the present time the Commission does not routinely meet with all Health Commissioning Agencies: rather it will arrange to meet specific agencies where issues of concern arising from a visit can be usefully pursued in this way. Overall the response from Health Commissioning Agencies to approaches from the Commission has been extremely positive and, on a number of occasions, it has facilitated the resolution of Commission concerns.

In the next two years the Commission will routinely be notifying all Health Commissioners in advance of visits to relevant provider units and, in consultation with the NHS Executive, it will seek to develop more routine contact with Health Commissioning Agencies on a regional basis, thereby ensuring that the particular needs of detained patients are central to those responsible for purchasing healthcare.

At a more general level the Commission, in collaboration with a number of Health Commissioning Agencies, has developed a guidance pack for purchasers about the Mental Health Act and the Code of Practice with suggested issues for monitoring and measures of performance. It is intended to publish this before the end of the year.

Section III

9 *Hospital Issues*

9.1   Role of the Hospital Managers

This topic is considered in Chapter 3.7.

9.2   Ward Environments

Environment

There are some excellent new facilities and many wards have been upgraded. Where the future of a hospital or ward within a hospital is uncertain, or is designated for closure, there is a tendency to allow the environment to deteriorate below an acceptable level. There are still some very impoverished environments, although generally standards have improved.

Dorothy Watkinson Unit, St Clements, Bow

Three side rooms in this unit had no adequate ventilation, no windows to the exterior and extremely poor decor and equipment. The Commission concluded that such conditions were unacceptable for the care of detained patients.

The hospital responded : "Unfortunately it is impossible to create windows in the three side rooms in this unit as the rooms back onto another ward. The ventilation problems are being rectified and the rooms redecorated. The service is currently investigating possible options on the St Clements site for relocating the unit".

It is not practicable to list all good new developments. Examples of imaginative refurbishment of existing wards include Rushmere Ward at St. Clement's Hospital, Ipswich and Severall's House at Severalls Hospital, North East Essex Mental Health NHS Trust. A number of excellent new facilities have also been created, for example, The George McKenzie High Dependency Unit at Fulbourn Hospital, Cambridge.

Staffing

Some hospitals have improved the level of trained nurses, others have low numbers of qualified staff. There is still a great reliance on bank nurses in some hospitals. There appears to be a growing shortage of trained nursing staff.

Staff morale is often found to be low in units which are due for closure and where ward conditions have deteriorated, placing staff under intense pressures. In contrast, even in wards where the degree of refurbishment still leaves considerable room for improvement, Commission members have found high levels of staff morale seemingly arising from extremely good, multidisciplinary team working between all professional staff in the unit, including doctors, nursing team and social workers (e.g. Willow House at Severall's Hospital).

In every area the decline in the occupational therapy service is reported with a diminution of the service and availability of these professionals. In part this appears to be due to a national shortage of such qualified professionals. Similarly, there appears to be a national shortage of psychologists and staff shortages are reported to members of the Commission as contributing to heavy workloads on nursing and other staff, leading to stress which cannot be helpful to patients with mental illness.

In some areas there seems to be a heavy pressure on psychiatrists also, particularly in relation to forensic psychiatry. If these problems are not addressed then there will inevitably be a gradual decline in the level and quality of the psychiatric services provided.

It is very apparent in some localities that the number of staff from black and ethnic communities does not reflect the proportion of black patients from such communities within the catchment area of that hospital. This may be considered to be unhelpful in diminishing the perceived lack of awareness of black ethnic issues in psychiatric hospitals.

Patient Mix

Two situations have been identified as matters of concern: the situation where adolescents are being treated on adult acute wards, especially where drug misuse is involved (see also Chapters 7.1 & 9.6) and the environments in which a number of women patients are placed (see Chapter 8.4).

9.3   Bed Occupancy and Extra-Contractual Referrals

Bed Shortages

The Commission's concern for the welfare of detained patients who have to be admitted to and treated in over-full admission wards was highlighted in its last Biennial Report. These concerns have persisted over the last two years and are not confined to London or other urban areas. These continued pressures on acute hospital beds cause additional strains upon the services which can be provided, on staff and on staff morale. Occupancy levels of 100% and above have been reported from areas of Devon, East Anglia and Cheshire as well as all the main conurbations. The situation is reported to be worse during the week than at weekends, when patients go on leave. However, filling leave beds is reported to create another problem in that patients on leave for the weekend can return on Monday morning to find their beds filled over the weekend by new admissions.

The situation reported in the last Biennial Report has worsened in the London and Manchester areas and average bed occupancies of about 130% are reported on occasion in some inner city hospitals. Many of those patients needing beds in acute wards are thought to be "the revolving door regulars of acute wards" [14].

Another general problem resulting from high bed occupancy is unavailability of beds at short notice for patients under Section 47/49 being transferred out from prison for rehabilitation within local Community Care settings.

An example of the difficulty in an urban Trust is illustrated in the box below.

Bed Occupancy at North Manchester Healthcare NHS Trust

The acute unit of North Manchester General Hospital continually operates at a 90% and over bed occupancy rate. This means that the unit is frequently closed to acute admissions. Persons seeking admission to the unit are often outposted to other in-patient units on the fringes of the Manchester area, or even further away. Beds occupied by patients on leave are often used for admission, and on occasions in-patients have been subject to early discharge to free beds for acute admissions. The Commission notes that these practices have a negative effect on both patients and staff.

There are several identified factors which play some part and they illustrate that the problem is not entirely one of decreased bed numbers.

Contributory factors include:

- identification of new, previously undetected, cases requiring hospital care by new Community Mental Health Teams

- bed-blocking of acute beds by under-resourced Community Care, particularly lack of 24 hour nursed beds and move-on accommodation

- reduced bed numbers and hospital closures in re-provision schemes

- an underestimated requirement for additional acute beds for people with chronic severe mental illness who have been successfully assimilated into community programs for rehabilitation but who nonetheless may continue to have acute relapses from time to time [15]. This underestimate may be due in part to an increased rate of relapse, coupled with a reduced duration of admission [16].

- In some parts of the country, e.g. Canterbury and Thanet Community Health Care NHS Trust and Addenbooke's NHS Trust in Cambridge, the Commission has received reports that there is an increasing placement of vulnerable people into residential care in their catchment areas from elsewhere in the country. These out of district placements in turn have a significant impact on the services available to the local populations (see Section IV for further discussion).

- In London, the report prepared by the Mental health Task Force considered that homelessness may contribute to the problem [17].

The consequences of the pressure on acute beds are an increasing number of extra-contractual referrals (ECRs), early discharges, and transfer of patients between hospitals within a short period of time. Many units describe themselves as "stretched beyond capacity." The general absence of crisis services continues to pose problems in many areas. There have been some developments but these are few and tentative.

The number of formal admissions under the Mental Health Act has increased dramatically by 31% in the period from 1987-88 to 1992-93, with most of the rise [18] due to admissions under Section 2 or 3 of the Act. This may be related to the observation that levels of disturbed behaviour in a number of acute facilities continue to rise, with great pressure being placed on the few units with higher levels of security which do exist to take patients as ECRs. Some Health Authorities are actively considering setting up secure "Special Care" facilities but are finding that the necessary funding is posing problems. There is also a reported increased use of the private sector in some areas.

Hollander and Slater [19] have published a study in the North East Thames Regional Health Authority which covers the north east part of London and the whole of Essex, serving a population of 3.8 million, the fourth largest in England and Wales, comprising 15 district health authorities. The study gives detailed statistics and shows that in 32% of 327 episodes of difficulty in finding a bed the patient could not be admitted, the remainder being admitted to a leave bed. Twelve per cent of the patients were described as particularly ill and five absconded during the search for a bed. Of the 22 patients who were not admitted to hospital, two were aggressive and eight were suicidal. The authors report considerable under-reporting of the problem. The authors highlight the need for continuing urgent attention to this matter, which the Mental Health Act Commissions finds still persists at this time.

> *The following examples illustrate some of the difficulties and the consequences for the patient when beds are not available:*
>
> *1. On 22nd May 1995 Mr A was involved as the patient in a Section 3 application by the Approved Social Worker. The application could not be completed as no secure bed could be found and the staff at the hospital would not nurse the patient in an insecure location. Consequently, Mr A was taken to the police station and held there because of a breach of the peace. Inquiries throughout the country failed to produce a bed. Eventually the staff at the hospital agreed to nurse Mr A, provided that the police remained on the ward until he was sedated. They did this. Mr A was detained at the hospital until 24th May at which time a bed was made available at an RSU.*
>
> *2. Mr M had been in seclusion since the beginning of the week. He was very difficult to handle, being a well-built 6ft 5 inches tall martial arts expert. On Monday he smashed the door of the seclusion room and police assistance was required. The room was subsequently barricaded with table tops and he was medicated with chlorpromazine, droperidol and lorazepam. The staff are all well-trained in control and restraint techniques and the Trust was concerned about the "inhumane" manner in which this patient was being cared for because no suitable facility could be found.*
>
> *The Trust made continuous attempts to find a medium secure bed for this man, without success. Where beds were available, staff problems meant that the location concerned still could not nurse him. An approach was made to Broadmoor Hospital without success.*
>
> *Mr M was finally moved to a newly opened RSU when it opened the following week: he was heavily sedated at the time of transfer.*

Regional Secure Units and High Dependency Units

The increased supply of beds in secure, medium secure and high dependency care is welcomed by the Commission. The Commission regularly receives reports from its visits that the pressure on the provision of acute beds still leads to additional pressures on the already overstretched secure facilities in Regional Secure Units.

To some extent this has been alleviated recently by the opening of more new medium secure and high dependency facilities. Several of the new facilities allocate only a proportion, sometimes only a relatively small proportion, of the total beds to the local population and rely upon ECRs to generate income to make them viable. Whilst sound financial management is to be commended, the new perspective could lead to the situation in which the local catchment area benefits less than would be expected by the opening of a new facility.

9.4 The Use of Section 17 Leave

Introduction

Section 17 of the Act requires the RMO to authorise personally any leave from hospital of a patient detained under the Act. This applies to any absence from the hospital or its grounds for any period of time, no matter how short that may be. Leave is usually granted subject to conditions which the RMO considers necessary in the interests of the patient or for the protection of other persons. There is considerable misunderstanding of the requirements of Section 17 of the Act. Many still believe, incorrectly, that a detained patient may go on leave without the completion of Section 17 leave formalities if they are only going out of the hospital grounds for a short while or if they are escorted by staff.

It needs to be emphasised that a detained patient can only lawfully leave the hospital where he/she is detained by:

- discharge
- lapse of the authority to detain
- transfer
- leave of absence can be granted by the Responsible Medical Officer (RMO) under Section 17 for specific occasions, such as attendance at a wedding, or out-patient hospital appointment, or for either definite or unspecified periods of time. The period of leave can be extended in the patient's absence.

There is no authority under the Act for the RMO to delegate his power to grant leave under Section 17. The RMO may attach any conditions to authorised leave that are deemed appropriate, such as limiting it to shopping expeditions or to home visits. Repeated periods of leave may also be authorised for specific purposes over a limited or unlimited period. The RMO may instruct nursing staff not to implement any authorised leave on medical grounds at their discretion.

The Section 17 leave form in use at Heron Lodge (Norfolk Mental Health Trust) includes the words "in the event of a patient's mental health deteriorating, leave may be curtailed at the discretion of the nurse in charge. Ref Code of Practice 20.4. "

The Commission considers it bad practice for nursing staff to withhold authorised Section 17 leave for any reason except a deterioration in the mental state of the patient. One example was encountered by Commission members in which a patient complained that his authorised leave was withheld because he would not attend ward community meetings.

The responsibility and accountability for Section 17 leave resides with the RMO. Commission members are increasingly asked whether the role of the RMO can be delegated to another doctor more directly involved in the care of the patient in the community, for example, the doctor involved in providing care to patients on leave in Registered Mental Nursing Homes or residential care homes. It is quite clear that this is not permissible under the Act, and transfer of responsibility can only be effected if the designated RMO changes.

The legislative history of Section 17 is described at pages 118 to 120 of "The Falling Shadow" [20].

Extended Leave of Absence under Section 17

Section 17 applies to the shortest period of absence, and also extended leave (up to 6 months for unrestricted patients). This will be increased to 12 months if the Mental Health (Patients in the Community) Bill is enacted. Trial leave is often used to assess suitability for discharge from section.

The provisions of Section 17 apply, without modification, to all patients subject to hospital and guardianship orders. It also applies with modification to restricted patients, when the approval of the Home Secretary is required. Section 17 leave lapses when the Section expires but a patient cannot be recalled from leave covered by Section 17 in order to renew detention under a Section of the Mental Health Act.

Care of the Patient whilst on Leave

Patients on Section 17 leave remain subject to the consent to treatment provisions of Part IV of the Mental Health Act (see Chapter 5). If it becomes necessary to administer treatment in the absence of the patient's consent under

Part IV, the patient should be recalled to hospital, the RMO being satisfied that recall is necessary in the interests of the patient's health or safety or for the protection of other persons.

The Code of Practice stresses (para 20.4) that the RMO and other professionals should be aware that their responsibilities for the patient's care remain the same whilst the patient is on leave, although they may be exercised in a different way.

Patients on leave are also subject to the aftercare provisions of Section 117.

Patients in Custody Whilst on Section 17 Leave

The RMO may direct that the patient remain in custody during the leave of absence if this is in the best interests of the patient, or for the protection of other persons. The patient may be kept in the custody of any officer on the staff of the hospital or of any person authorised in writing by the Hospital Managers. These sorts of arrangements are often useful, for example, to allow patients to participate in escorted trips but with a requirement to remain in custody throughout, or to have compassionate home leave.

If, as a condition of leave, the patient is to reside in a different hospital, responsibility for the custody of the patient can be given to a officer on the staff of that hospital. Such an officer need be neither a nurse nor a doctor. However, a patient on Section 17 leave from one hospital to a second hospital remains liable to be detained at the first hospital. In Mental Health Act terms the patient is not detained at the second hospital, although, as noted above, the patient may be in the custody of an officer of the second hospital.

Commission Concerns About the Use of Section 17

Over the years, the Commission has expressed various concerns about the use of the Section 17 power. The Commission wishes to draw particular attention to the fact that the power of the RMO to grant leave to a patient to be absent from hospital may be currently misused. It is being used, not for leave of absence properly so described, but as a substitute for transfer from one hospital to another under Section 19. In the 4th Biennial Report (paragraph 9.7 - page 38), the Commission described the situation, in the context of moves from district hospital to RSUs as follows:

In other cases Section 17 has been used to move a patient presenting severe management problems from a district hospital to an RSU. A limited period of intensive care at the RSU is then followed by return to the district hospital where the patient has remained liable to be detained. It is the Commission's view that such a procedure is contrary to the intentions of Section 17. Inevitably the move takes place during an acute phase of mental disorder and removes the patient from easy access to his RMO and managers under the Act at the district hospital, who have specific powers regarding consent to treatment and discharge. At such a time, the patient cannot be involved in the decision for leave, as recommended by the Code of Practice. The root cause of the use of Section 17 in this way lies in the reluctance of some district hospitals to accept the return of particular difficult patients once transferred out of their care and in inability of RSUs to offer long-term care. In the long run, the establishment of long-term care facilities for difficult-to-manage patients is required for every district. Meanwhile, a standard transfer of full care to the RSU for limited time is preferable to the use of Section 17 leave which gives the patient both necessary treatment and maximum protection of rights under the Act.

The Commission is concerned that, for some patients, Section 17 is being used to move them from a Special Hospital to a RSU where they may remain for months or even years in circumstances where transfer would be more appropriate.

The Commission recognises that trial leave may include periods of stay at another hospital: indeed this is recognised in Section 17(3). It is the duration of such so-called trial leave, and its inappropriate use in circumstances when the patient is in fact being, or should be, transferred to the other hospital, which calls for further investigation and consideration. The Commission does not have detailed statistical information, but suspects that the practice is widespread, and not confined to movements of patients from Special Hospitals, but extends, for example, to the movement of patients from NHS hospitals to medium secure Registered Mental Nursing Homes.

The disadvantages for the patient, where the trial leave is long-term, appear to the Commission to be as follows :

- The RMO at the Special Hospital remains responsible for the patient. For example, the RMO retains powers and duties under Section 17(4), Section 20(3), Section 41(6) and Section 58 (these statutory references ignore the distinction between restricted and non-restricted patients). This statutory responsibility does not sit comfortably with the fact that the RMO is no longer in charge of the treatment of the patient (compare the definition of "responsible medical officer" in Section 55(1)).

- The patient on extended trial leave, but confined to another hospital, may be many miles from his original hospital - in such cases, his RMO is unlikely to visit on any regular basis.

- There are examples of situations where unrestricted patients have been sent on trial leave to another hospital with the RMO directing that the patient remain in the custody of an officer on the staff of the receiving hospital, as permitted under Section 17(3), or where the patient has remained at the receiving hospital after the authority to detain at the original hospital has expired. In both these cases, the Commission is concerned that the patient is being detained, or has been detained, wrongfully.

9.5   Use of Seclusion

Seclusion is now used to a far lesser extent than it was a few years ago. In some hospitals its use has been discontinued. Other Trusts which do still use it are aiming either to reduce it or to phase it out. This has been helped by the introduction of identified primary nurses. It may be however, that the number of locked wards is increasing. They may be designated as unlocked, but they are frequently locked because there are high-risk patients present. Seclusion is discussed in relation to Registered Mental Nursing Homes in Chapter 9.7 and in relation to Special Hospitals in Chapter 9.8.

9.6   Use of Illicit Drugs

The misuse of drugs appears to be a growing problem in all types of mental health services. Drug misuse poses particularly acute problems for in-patient psychiatric services. In a recent survey by the Royal College of Nursing for the BBC, 70% of respondents (187), from both urban and rural areas, said that the misuse of illicit drugs was a problem in their unit. Only half of these units had a policy in relation to patients who use illicit drugs.

Members of the Mental Health Act Commission report that it is becoming increasingly common for drug misuse to be raised as a concern in units visited. They also report general concern about the limited specialist services available to patients who have these problems. There are also widespread concerns about the integration of patients who abuse drugs (both illicit drugs and alcohol) with other mentally ill patients.

It may be the appropriate time to give special consideration to the complex legal, ethical and medical issues raised by the misuse of drugs in psychiatric services. It is a problem that has already been confronted by drug dependency units, many of which have formulated policies to address the situation, including the use of patient 'contracts'.

Although it seems likely that visitors are the chief source of supply, there is as yet very little hard evidence about the scale or nature of drug misuse in these settings or about the types of drugs misused, although there are indications that cannabis presents the major problem in terms of frequency of abuse. Other 'hard' drugs are encountered less frequently but may be more deleterious to mental well-being than cannabis.

Issues which arise include:

- the rights of voluntary and involuntary patients
- the limitations which can be imposed on detained patients in contracts
- the rights of visitors
- the authority of hospital personnel to conduct searches
- the need for and the limits to co-operation with the police
- the relative importance to be attached to different drugs of abuse in relation to their effects upon mental disorders and their interaction with medication
- differential harmful effects of drugs of abuse on patients receiving medication compared with others in the community who are not in receipt of such medication
- the difficulties in devising policies in an in-patient setting such as the use of incentives or loss of privileges.

There is a clear need to train staff in general issues surrounding substance misuse and about the effect of these substances on health and mental health.

There is a pressing need for research to determine the extent and nature of the problem and into effective solutions, as well as a more immediate need to develop guidance in producing a framework for the development of local policies.

It would be helpful for some input from the Department of Health on these matters so that hospitals can develop policies which not only alleviate the problem but do so in a manner which conforms to current ethics and standards.

The problems and literature associated with the consumption of illicit drugs within a Special Hospital have been highlighted from a staff perspective in a recent paper based on findings at Ashworth Hospital[21]. The report states that the most common illicit drug is cannabis and that the staff perception of the use of other drugs including amphetamines, LSD, Valium, Ecstasy, magic mushrooms and alcohol was minimal. Staff concluded that illicit drugs caused a *"general deterioration of mental health or exacerbation of existing problems....increased*

*aggression and violent behaviour in some patients misusing drugs.. with
increased conflict between staff and patients and amongst patients themselves"*.
However, it must be stressed that these are staff perceptions of the problems
rather than quantitative reporting of factual research data concerning use and the
consequences of use. Nevertheless, some of the recommendations have inherent
sense and these include education and training of staff, patients and visitors with
respect to drug misuse and a raised awareness of the issues. Some
recommendations regarding security are also proffered but it is clear that there is
no clear agreement on the efficacy of such measures.

Within less secure environments the problems are somewhat different, with a
greater difficulty in preventing the influx of illicit drugs into the hospital.
Members of the Commission are often asked for their views on the measures
which can be taken or on policies to be developed. However, the Commission
does not have a precise view on the matter except as stated above, namely, that
the nature and magnitude of the problem needs objective and impartial
investigation. The problem then needs to be restated. Then, and only then, can a
rational and consistent approach to policy be developed.

9.7   Medium Secure Registered Mental Nursing Homes

With the closure of the large psychiatric hospitals, many Health Authorities have
experienced a shortage of medium secure facilities. This has resulted in an
increase in a number of detained patients funded by their Health Authorities or
NHS Trusts in medium secure Registered Mental Nursing Homes, often at a
significant distance from their home area. The Commission visits five such
hospitals. Four are owned by Partnerships in Care (Stockton Hall, Llanarth Court,
St John's and Kneesworth House Hospital) the fifth is St Andrew's Hospital in
Northampton. These five facilities provide care for a considerable proportion of
detained patients at any one time. This makes them significant providers in their
own right and is the justification for their inclusion in this way in the report.

It is important to emphasise that they provide care for many very disturbed
patients for whom the NHS has no appropriate provision and the significance of
the independent sector's contribution to the provision of mental health secure
care cannot be over emphasised. It is also important to recognise that a number
of the issues referred to below are equally applicable to many NHS facilities.
These hospitals are visited quarterly or biannually by members of the Commission
who also make unannounced visits. The concerns set out below do not
necessarily refer to all the Registered Mental Nursing Homes visited and, in order
to present a balanced picture it is appropriate to report that members of the

Commission visit many wards in private Registered Mental Nursing Homes offering impressive amenities and care, including good general provision and private rooms, high standards of furnishing and regular, detailed reviews of care, with excellent documentation procedures.

The Registering Authorities

The Commission has become increasingly concerned that the statutory framework and the criteria used by the registering authorities (the local District Health Authority) for these hospitals may not be adequate to cover the type of patient that is generally received. Particular concern centres on staffing requirements which for the majority of Registered Mental Nursing Homes may be adequate, but for the hospitals under consideration may be at times insufficient, given the severity of illness and the challenging nature of the patients detained.

In only one instance has the Commission been approached by a registering authority regarding a proposal to open a new facility. In making comments on the proposal the Commission was able to raise awareness with the licensing authority on matters of concern that fall within its remit. The Commission will be advising the Department to review current criteria to take into account the very specific challenges presented by detained patients within these units.

Standards of Care

Arrangements for monitoring standards of care given to NHS patients in Registered Mental Nursing Homes is a matter for the NHS body purchasing the care and the mental nursing home as well as, by virtue of its duties under the Registered Homes Act 1984, the relevant registering authority.

It is the Commission's perception that unlike within the NHS, the use of the contractual process to develop standards in this sector has been minimal and the Commission is aware of the unhappiness felt by a number of Registered Mental Nursing Homes at the lack of positive interest displayed by some purchasing NHS authorities once a patient has been placed with them. There are a number of barriers to the more creative use of the contractual process including:

- a very large number of purchasers use each Registered Mental Nursing Home
- there is no "lead" purchaser
- many homes rely on the licensing authorities to maintain standards
- required standards of care may vary considerably.

As the contractual process is one of the most important factors in determining standards, the Commission believes that it should have a role in advising purchasers regarding required standards and the means by which purchasing bodies can ensure that they are attained. To this end, the Mental Health Act Commission is developing a range of standards, and related performance indicators, which are based on the revised Code of Practice. When finalised, the standards and performance indicators will be circulated to all Health Authorities.

Mental Health Act Managers

Under the Act, "the Managers" in relation to a Registered Mental Nursing Home are the persons registered (under the Registered Homes Act) in respect of the home. The Managers have a number of important statutory responsibilities (see Chapter 24 - Code of Practice) including reviewing renewals of detention (Section 20) and exercising their power to discharge (Section 23).

The Commission is pleased that these responsibilities have been delegated to committees of persons independent of the hospitals, in line with earlier Commission advice. The Commission is concerned that the naming of these committees should not be such as to cause patients to confuse them with Mental Health Review Tribunals. For example, the term "Review Panel" may not be helpful in this respect.

The Managers' other responsibilities are currently delegated to officers of the nursing home, as in many NHS Trusts. Whilst such delegation must be accompanied by clear lines of accountability, it is the Commission's view (applicable to both the NHS and independent sectors) that the independent persons, appointed as above, can frequently also make a useful and constructive contribution to monitoring the implementation of the other duties of the Managers (for example, in ensuring that the grounds for admitting the patient are valid) as well as being encouraged to take a constructive and appropriate interest in the general provision of care to detained patients.

Such involvement is not always appropriate or possible but the advantages that it can offer to maintaining high standards, especially in relation to the observation of rights and provision of care to detained patients is worthy of active consideration.

Admissions

It has been noted that some patients are admitted to the hospitals on Section 17 leave. The rationale for its use lies in the fact that it guarantees the return of the patient should the placement be unsatisfactory.

From the patient's perspective, the use of Section 17 leave means that his/her Responsible Medical Officer and 'the Managers' to whom appeals can be made remain at the referring hospital. Leave cannot be renewed after 6 months. A patient cannot be recalled from leave in order to renew the authority to detain the patient.

The use of Section 17 leave to transfer detained patients to these hospitals is highly unsatisfactory. Instances are known where leave has been renewed without the patients being recalled to the referring hospital. Representation on this practice has been made to the Department of Health.

Patients Subject to a Transfer Directive - Section 47 - 49

The difficulties attached to the failure of the Act to empower the Home Secretary to direct the transfer of a mentally disordered prisoner direct to a Registered Mental Nursing Home has already been noted. (Chapter 3.11). This deficiency is circumvented by ordering the transfer of the patient to an NHS hospital from which they are immediately transferred to the Registered Mental Nursing Home under Section 19. Whilst such arrangements are undertaken in good faith and in the interests of the patient, it is unfortunate that such transfers have to be effected in this artificial way and the Commission would welcome an amendment to the Act.

Adherence to the Code of Practice

Seclusion

The Commission has long been concerned that practices regarding seclusion have not always conformed with the Code of Practice in Registered Mental Nursing Homes. The difficulties arise, in part, from the fact that the hospitals do not always have residential 24 hour medical cover, and that the use of seclusion is viewed as a beneficial form of treatment for their particularly difficult group of patients.

Generally there are good records kept of seclusion and policies are adhered to. However, there tends to be a higher use in the more secure environments for patients with learning disabilities or mental disabilities acquired through brain injury. To some extent, the continued use of seclusion for these patients is based upon historical accident and relationships within the hospitals, professional isolation and ingrained beliefs, which often may not be founded upon sound clinical research or impartial ethical judgement [22].

The Code of Practice 18.17 stipulates that the decision to use seclusion can be made in the first instance by a doctor, the nurse in charge of the ward, a nursing officer or senior nursing officer. Where the decision is taken by someone other than a doctor, then the necessary arrangements must be made for a doctor to attend immediately.

At St Andrew's Hospital, the RMO or duty doctor is informed when a patient remains in seclusion for 30 minutes. However, the doctor often does not attend and there have been instances of patients remaining in seclusion for periods in excess of one hour without seeing a doctor. At Kneesworth House Hospital the RMO or his deputy is expected to attend whenever possible at the 45 minute interval. After two hours, attendance by the patient's RMO, or his deputy, is mandatory. Commission members have continually raised their concern about these practices. Resistance to the implementation of the guidance is, however, strong as it is thought impracticable. At Kneesworth House Hospital, the Commission has been informed that 90% of all seclusions terminate within 10 minutes. Within the Kemsley Division at St Andrew's, it is argued that the practice of seclusion (from 2 - 40 minutes) is integral to the behaviour modification programmes.

The Commission remains dissatisfied with these current hospital practices. Not only is the guidance frequently breached, but the lack of 24 hour medical cover means that patients within the hospitals can be considered to be at 'high risk'.

The early involvement of a patient's doctor, or his deputy, not only appropriately marks the significance of placing someone in seclusion, but leads to early evaluation of its continuation and adds a professional component to the nursing perspective. The Commission will therefore continue to press for the full implementation of the guidance in the Code of Practice in each of the hospitals.

Other Commission concerns relate to the failure to provide sufficient privacy, including examples of more than one patient being locked in a room together. This is not seclusion as defined in the Code of Practice and the Commission is concerned about the practice for the safety of patients, as it is not subject to the same recording and monitoring requirements as seclusion policy in the Code of Practice. Seclusion is sometimes used as part of a patient's treatment plan where inadequate recording procedures have been noted. There has been a continual failure to address some identified physical hazards in the seclusion rooms.

At Kneesworth House Hospital statistical data on the use of seclusion have now been provided. The Commission has been assured that regular monitoring occurs throughout the 24 hour clinical ward reviews but clear documentation is lacking to support this assurance.

Section 117 Aftercare

In all the hospitals, the difficulties in maintaining contact with a referring authority once a patient has been admitted, is of concern both to the Commission and the hospitals concerned. Once a patient is considered to be approaching discharge a request is made to the referring authority to attend a Section 117 meeting. Requests are also made to attend reviews. It is often reported to the Commission that local authorities refuse to send representatives to the meeting. When this occurs Section 117 arrangements are made by correspondence. The Commission believes this to be unsatisfactory and that the hospital's lack of detailed information regarding the patient's local facilities to which he/she will return severely disadvantages the patient.

The timing of aftercare meetings remains problematic. Meetings are often left until a patient is ready for discharge. The Commission has recommended early Section 117 meetings in case a patient is discharged by the Managers or the Mental Health Review Tribunal. A complaint at one of the hospitals is currently under investigation, where such a discharge occurred and the patient, despite attempts by the hospital to involve the local authority, was discharged without adequate support in the community being in place.

Ward Environments

Concerns are regularly expressed concerning the patient mix on wards. It is not unusual for patients diagnosed with mental illness to be accommodated on a ward with patients who are diagnosed as psychopathic or severely mentally impaired. The Commission considers that this places vulnerable people, especially those who are who are severely mentally impaired, at risk. The age range of patients on the wards is often undesirable.

Overcrowding of wards is a common concern to the Commission. In Kneesworth House Hospital wards have 34 beds, which is considered to be out of step with current NHS practice. Some wards do not have sufficient chairs and it is usual for meals to be taken in shifts. At St Andrew's Hospital the inappropriate patient mix and the observed poor staff/patient interaction has led to the establishment of an attention seeking culture by patients, who feel neglected.

Access to outside exercise is often limited. Access may be dependent upon whether a patient has been granted parole, and the availability of staff to escort and monitor patients when outside. It is often the patient's perception that staff are generally too busy to guarantee the honouring of parole arrangements.

General Physical Care

Commission members have expressed concerns about the physical care given to patients. Inspection of patients' medical files have shown that general physical examinations are not regularly given upon admission, or if given not repeated, despite many of the patients having poor physical medical histories. Patients are registered with local General Practitioners. It is felt that this arrangement has led to a split in physical and psychiatric care that is not found in NHS Trust hospitals. At Kneesworth House Hospital, the integration of the respective files is poor, often resulting in unsatisfactory continuing care. The monitoring of known physical conditions of patients leaves much to be desired.

Behaviour Modification Programmes

At St Andrew's Hospital, patients with widely varying characteristics, including the acutely psychiatrically ill, those with acquired brain damage requiring rehabilitation and adolescents, have been subject to a standard group of ward behaviour modification practices. There have been some improvements in these programmes in line with Commission comments but on some wards the programme focus is perceived by patients as predominantly negative with an emphasis on unacceptable behaviour and non-compliance leading to loss of earnings. In many cases the programme does not address individual problems and despite regular reviews many patients remain for lengthy periods on ward programmes which do not apparently result in significant behavioural change.

Advocacy

The Commission is pleased to report that all the hospitals appear to be either establishing independent advocacy or are examining the possibility.

St Andrew's now employs an advocacy worker and intends to establish a Patients' Council. Llanarth Court is hoping to arrange advocacy in conjunction with Gwent MIND. Kneesworth House Hospital is exploring possible advocacy services.

Supervision Register

All hospitals have indicated problems, similar to those encountered with Section 117 (Chapters 3.10 and 10.2), in liaising with referring authorities on matters relating to the Supervision Register.

9.8 Visiting Special Hospitals

Introduction

The Commission devotes a considerable amount of its resources to its work in the three Special Hospitals. These hospitals continue to provide care and treatment for approximately 1600 patients detained under the Mental Health Act. Most of these patients are detained under Part III of the Act as the consequence of criminal proceedings but approximately one-fifth are subject to civil detention.

The Department of Health Working Group examining the future of high security care was established in 1992. It reported to Ministers in April 1993 and was published in 1994. In June 1995, Ministers were able to announce the future management arrangements for the Special Hospitals. This long period of uncertainty for those working in the Special Hospitals inevitably was unfortunate and led to representations being made to Ministers during this time.

The Special Health Services Authority (SHSA) will cease to exist after 31 March 1996, and will be replaced by a National High Security Psychiatric Services Commissioning Board, responsible for commissioning services provided by the Special Hospitals. The hospitals themselves become individual Special Health Authorities in their own right.

The Commissioning Board is a committee within the NHS Executive and is responsible to the NHS Chief Executive. In addition to purchasing services from the Special Hospitals, it also seems likely that it will have an important role in the strategic planning of long-term medium secure care.

The Commission welcomes the end to the uncertainty about the future of the Special Hospitals and strongly supports the expressed intention of Ministers to "ensure the most effective deployment of the full range of services according to patients' needs".

The Collaboration Between the Mental Health Act Commission and Special Health Services Authority on Special Hospitals Quality Standards

In May 1995 the Commission and the SHSA agreed to collaborate over the setting and monitoring of quality standards in Special Hospitals.

Each year the Authority enters into a service level agreement with each hospital which includes key quality standards to be monitored. As the Commission is also concerned with issues of quality relating to the Mental Health Act, it has been agreed that it would be highly desirable to collaborate.

Under the agreement:

- at the beginning of each SHSA quality standard review year, both parties will discuss the key quality standards to be included in the service level agreements for the forthcoming year

- the Commission will devote part of its visiting resources to examine an aspect, or aspects of one or more of the SHSA quality standards which fall within the Commission's statutory remit

- a liaison cycle will be developed consistent with the SHSA quality standard monitoring and review cycle and both organisations will share the outcome of the monitoring.

It is the Commission's view that such collaboration will enable it to pursue its remit more effectively and will point the way to possible future ways of collaborating with other NHS purchasers. When the Commissioning Board replaces the SHSA it is hoped to continue this collaboration.

In the 5 years of its life, the SHSA has secured major beneficial changes in the provision of Special Hospital care and has introduced modern systems of management and monitoring which should provide a firm foundation for the future. In particular it is appropriate to highlight:-

- the elimination of slopping out and the introduction of 24 hour therapeutic care

- the implementation of an authority-wide seclusion policy.

- the increased priority given to aftercare and patient transfer

- the introduction of ward managers

- the implementation of an authority-wide complaints policy

A great deal remains to be done, much of which is identified later in this chapter. Notwithstanding, these are important achievements and it is right that they are recognised.

It is inevitable that the relationship between a service provider and the organisation charged with monitoring aspects of its work will not always run smoothly and the relationship between the Commission and the SHSA has been no exception. Notwithstanding the occasional vigour of the debate, neither organisation ever doubted the seriousness and integrity with which the other pursued its responsibilities and it has been in that context that the Commission believes the dialogue of the last 5 years has made a genuine contribution to improving the care and treatment of Special Hospital patients. The Commission would therefore like to place on record its appreciation of the work of the SHSA and the manner in which it has conducted its relationship with the Commission.

Environmental Standards

24 Hour Care

Significant progress has been made towards the full introduction of 24 hour therapeutic care with open access for patients to their own rooms or dormitories. Rampton Hospital has completed implementation. The resulting increase in patient choice and freedom of movement within each residential area has been the subject of positive comment by many patients to members of the Commission.

To obtain all the benefits, therapeutic and otherwise, that can flow from the new regime is challenging for all staff, particularly nurses for whom it should mean more extensive therapeutic engagement with their patients. The centrality of the role of the ward manager in focusing nursing care to achieve these benefits cannot be over-emphasised and the Commission has noted that such objectives are beginning to be achieved in parts of all three Special Hospitals.

Ward Environments

At **Rampton** Hospital the programme of refurbishment and upgrading of ward environments is continuing rapidly and the contrast with those wards that have not been upgraded is sometimes stark. The furnishings are poor on the wards not yet refurbished; in one location it was necessary to point out that the number and quality of easy chairs was unacceptable. A second, completely new block of three wards has been built within the hospital and came into use in 1994. Apart from some very minor adjustments, these new wards give excellent facilities for the patients who have taken up residence there.

Commission members have received complaints from both patients and staff about ward moves within the hospital in order to allow the refurbishment to take place. Patients have felt vulnerable and powerless to have any input into major changes affecting their lives and the environment in which they live, largely because of the manner in which patients have been notified of the moves and the subsequent way in which they were managed. Some patients have been subject to repeated moves and others have been left on their ward with the refurbishment work going on around them. The Commission made strong representation to the Hospital Management Team about these issues and sought assurance that future changes would be handled in a more sympathetic manner.

Sheridan Ward, the only mixed gender ward, nursing a large group of profoundly handicapped patients within the hospital, has presented major difficulties. It was decided to close this ward and to disperse those patients to other wards largely within the hospital. Commission members were particularly worried about this proposal, in case the facilities offered to those individuals from Sheridan Ward were inappropriate to meet their real needs. It was also considered that their adverse behaviour might have a detrimental effect on the patients within the receiving wards. The Commission indicated its view that this group of profoundly handicapped people might be better cared for in smaller, single gender units offering more individual care. Commission members continue to monitor very carefully these patient moves. They will also monitor the consequences for the patients who are moving and for the group they will join.

At **Broadmoor** Hospital the physical environment of Dorset House, comprising two large dormitories, greatly concerned Commission members and patients told Commission members that they were "afraid to sleep on the third floor". They complained that various unwelcome activities, including sexual acts, harassment, and assault went unchecked at night. As a result, some patients refused to sleep in the dormitory. Commission members reported that the ward was overcrowded and that environmental conditions were of an unacceptably low standard. The dormitories were supervised at night by five or six members of staff, ordinarily stationed outside the dormitories, who walked through at fixed times. It was reported that, between such visits, the staff occasionally observed the patients through the observation panels in the entrance doors, though there appeared to be no documentary evidence that this actually happened. To gain access to the sixteen-bed ward it was necessary for the staff to descend to the second floor and then climb the back stairs to the ward entrance. The arrangements were such that for extended periods during the night the patients on these wards appeared to be largely unobserved and unsupervised.

Commission members were also concerned that in the event of a fire it would be very difficult to achieve rapid evacuation of all the patients and staff. Commission members concluded that the prevailing arrangements on the third floor of Dorset House at night were dangerous both to patients and staff, and advised the Secretary of State of their concerns in March 1994. In November 1994, it was noted that there had been little improvement. Subsequently the Commission was delighted to be informed that the capital investment necessary to secure the closure of this facility and its complete refurbishment had been brought forward, together with additional revenue funding. The last patients left in March 1995 to newly refurbished ward environments. However, there are still wards with more than 20 patients and dormitories at Broadmoor Hospital. The Commission welcomes the SHSA's self-imposed standard that wards will not exceed 20 patients but this will require additional revenue as well as capital resources..

In **Ashworth** Hospital, organisational changes, similar to those in the other Special Hospitals, are resulting in patients being placed in one of four clinical areas; Mental Illness North and South, the Personality Disorder Unit or the Specialist Service Unit. Within this overall plan patients have sometimes found themselves moved more than once before reaching their eventual ward areas. Difficulties are emerging in relation to the Personality Disorder Units where there are clearly more patients than beds currently available (resulting in some patients being accommodated elsewhere) and Commission Members get the impression that nurses do not feel adequately trained to "manage" the often challenging behaviour of those patients. There have been problems with such patients being placed on inappropriate wards and causing disruption.

There are currently twenty or more patients on each Personality Disorder Ward. The view of the Commission is that such patients should be nursed on wards of ten to twelve patients but resources currently make achieving this target impossible. The Commission will be paying particular attention to the development of this unit within the next two years.

Lack of Access to Fresh Air

In the past two years the Commission has received numerous complaints from patients about difficulties in getting adequate access to fresh air. Such access is a very basic entitlement and the Commission welcomes the attention given to this matter by the SHSA and each hospital. Fresh air and exercise should be part of each patient's care plan and every ward is now required to audit such activity every month.

Many wards do not have their own gardens and not infrequently, where a group of patients do not want to take exercise, there are insufficient staff to care for them and also supervise those who do.

The Commission has a related concern that the excellent sports and recreational facilities in the hospitals are under used for a variety of reasons. For example, the swimming pool at Broadmoor Hospital was shut for most of the summer of 1994 and only opened again at the end of July 1995.

The provision of adequate access to fresh air and exercise must be accorded the highest priority in the next two years.

Transfer Delays

The Commission continues to be extremely concerned about the long delays in transferring patients from Special Hospitals to Regional Secure Units, local psychiatric hospitals or units or to community facilities.

During the period under review, there has been little significant improvement in the position, despite efforts to tackle the difficulties. Patients identified by clinical teams as suitable for discharge or transfer to less secure conditions, often including those patients who have been granted a conditional discharge by a Mental Health Review Tribunal, continue to be detained in an environment of maximum security which is inappropriate to their needs.

Within the three Special Hospitals the approach to transfer delays has become much more systematic, with improved monitoring of progress. The hospitals have begun a quarterly circulation to relevant Health Authorities, NHS Trusts and Social Service Departments of relevant details of the patients for whom they have responsibility. The Commission hopes that it will be possible to continue this practice. General Managers have become involved where delays last over six months. The Commission is provided with periodic reviews of patients awaiting transfer, including summary reports of current reasons for delay in individual cases. Where there are particular delays at a local level, Commission visiting teams for those particular Trusts are made aware of the transfer difficulties to ensure that they raise these matters and ascertain what plans local Trusts have to fulfil their obligations.

There are three main areas of difficulty in relation to patient transfers which are:

- Long waits for patients to be assessed for transfer to Regional Secure Units (RSUs), largely due to heavy demand on places from other referrers e.g. Courts. This is made more difficult if an onward route from the RSU is not identified and agreed before the placement starts

- Patchy provision at local level across the country, which means that the speed and quality of service offered to patients who no longer need maximum security is unpredictable. Patients with learning disability are particularly affected and the problem is exacerbated when there are no plans to provide suitable facilities or there are said to be no funds to purchase

- Some purchasers are relying on independent sector provision which is sometimes inappropriate for the needs of a particular individual and/or because it is isolating in terms of achieving successful rehabilitation into a person's home area

- Disputes between Health and Social Services about which Authorities should be responsible for, and therefore fund, any service to be offered

- In some cases, the time taken by the Home Office to decide whether to consent to a proposed transfer is very lengthy.

Seclusion

The Commission welcomes the introduction of the SHSA's policy on the use of seclusion and the alternative management of disturbed behaviour. The objective is to promote alternative approaches to the care and treatment of disturbed behaviour and to limit the use of seclusion to exceptional circumstances.

Seclusion for the purpose of this new policy is defined in accordance with the Mental Health Act Code of Practice which clearly states that its use is for the protection of others only. The introduction of privacy locks on patients' rooms, their right to privacy and the opportunity for time alone, if they wish, without being locked in their room will terminate the need for "self seclusion" together with other practices of confinement which previously existed and which did not comply with the Code of Practice.

Although considerable progress has been made in implementing fully this new policy, there are still some elements yet to be introduced. For example, at **Broadmoor** Hospital full implementation is dependent on the introduction of 24 hour therapeutic care on some of the wards where seclusion might need to be used. (See also Chapter 9.7 for use of seclusion in Registered Mental Nursing Homes). Members of the Commision have established that, even where 24 hour therapeutic care has been established, especially at night, regular reviews as required by the Code of Practice do not occur owing to staff shortages.

At **Rampton** Hospital the role of the doctor in reviewing any episode of seclusion cannot be fully implemented until extra recruitment of doctors enables there to be 24 hour on-site medical cover.

Commission members observed informally that staff appear not to have actually read the policy, are not wholly positive towards it. The programme of staff training clearly needs to continue.

On those wards where patients are exhibiting disturbed behaviour with the risk of harm to others or themselves, high staffing levels are required to maintain the appropriate intervention and levels of observation and to prevent the use of seclusion. The Commission is mindful of the effects this could have on the remaining patients on such a ward and carefully monitor that the staff levels are sufficient to avoid disadvantaging the on-going treatment plans for the remaining patients.

The three hospitals acknowledge the presence of a very small group of difficult patients who require periods of extended seclusion from time to time, which is not supported by guidance in the Code of Practice. The seclusion of these patients is monitored particularly closely by the Hospital Management Teams as well as by the Commission and is being separately recorded to ensure that an accurate statistical picture of the use of seclusion emerges.

Complaints

Since the introduction of the SHSA Complaints Policy to all three Special Hospitals there has been a considerable and welcome improvement in the investigation of patients' complaints. One consequence has been a decline in the number of complaints from Special Hospital patients that require Commission investigation. The Commission is given unrestricted access to data collected during complaints investigations by the Hospitals, and continues to examine a random selection of complaints files on a result basis. Commission Members have paid particular attention to the work of the Independent Investigators appointed under the Complaints Policy and have continued to note a wide variation in the quality of their work. These deficiencies have been drawn to the attention of the Special Hospitals. As a result, the Commission has been pleased to note the recruitment of a wider more representative group of professionals and the implementation of ongoing training.

The Commission's monitoring of Special Hospital complaints has identified some continuing problems;

- A failure in a number of cases to adhere to the time scales laid down in the policy. It is recognised that this can sometimes be due to the difficulties in making speedy appointments with witnesses but in other cases there is some evidence that staff who are the subject of or witnesses to matters complained about do not accord sufficiently high priority to responding to complaints investigations.

- A reluctance, in some cases, to pay compensation to patients where a finding of a complaints investigation would clearly warrant such payment.

Special Hospitals and Part IV of the Mental Health Act

Patients' RMOs have a responsibility to evaluate regularly whether or not patients are consenting to treatment. Should a patient withhold or withdraw consent or become incapable of giving valid consent, a Second Opinion from a doctor appointed by the Commission must be requested.

Commission members continue to monitor the Consent to Treatment provision of the Act (see also Chapter 4). At **Broadmoor** and **Ashworth** Hospitals there is some progress in compliance with the Act in relation to completion of consent Forms 38 and the quality of information. However, Commission members still have to draw attention to inadequately completed forms which do not comply with the Code of Practice. Except at **Rampton** Hospital, there is no systematic approach to the maintenance of consent forms to ensure that only the current consent form is the one with the patient's medicine card. The Commission has had to remind nurses that they are under an ethical and legal obligation to ensure that when they are administering treatment they are doing so lawfully.

Another major difficulty is the frequent change of the patients' RMOs and failure by some of the new RMOs to review patients' consent and to complete new consent forms, resulting in the use of forms which are obsolete. Commission members also have concerns that there is often no record of consent having been discussed and recorded in the clinical notes. This is very worrying if a consent to treatment form has been completed verifying the fact that the prescribed medication together with its likely effects has been discussed with the patient.

The Commission continues to recommend that the current consent form is kept with the patient's medicine card to ensure that the nurse administering the medication is confident that the drugs administered are within the limitations set out in the consent form agreed with the patient and that previous consent forms are either removed or clearly cancelled.

There remains a concern, certainly at **Ashworth** and **Broadmoor** Hospitals, about the over-medication of women patients.

At **Ashworth** hospital, the operation of Part IV of the Act has improved over the last year but there remain instances of patients moving from ward to ward in the reorganisation without the new RMO signing the patient's form 38.

At **Rampton** Hospital Commission members were surprised to learn that social workers very rarely act as the "other consultee" when a Second Opinion Appointed Doctor is assessing a patient's treatment plan, prior to issuing a certificate of Second Opinion. In view of the important role social workers have in clinical teams, it was suggested that the Social Work Department should review this situation and agree a policy with other professions within the hospital that would ensure that social workers' expertise is recognised in this matter.

Rehabilitation Services

At **Rampton** Hospital, as a result of discussions with patients and staff together with visits to off-ward areas, Commission members have found it necessary to bring to the attention of the Hospital Management Team and Hospital Advisory Committee, on a number of occasions, their concern about the adequacy of the current rehabilitation services.

Not only do patients feel that there has been a deterioration in the facilities offered during the day as part of a rehabilitation programme but they also feel that the organisation of the total service seems to be in some disarray. Patients indicate that they feel frustrated and are not getting the opportunity to express themselves appropriately. It has also been put to Commission members that some patients are bored, being unable to fill their day. Patients express the view that there is now insufficient activity to cater for the range of abilities in the hospital population. Some of the patients have indicated that they would like to have more opportunity to spend longer periods in the workshops and there is a feeling that attending an activity throughout the day and having lunch at the "workplace" would be more in line with real life situations. As a result of difficulties in keeping the escorting arrangements to time and the distances involved, many patients are only in their activity location for a very short period before being required to clear up and prepare to return to their ward for lunch, with the process repeated in the afternoon. This means that they are spending as much time waiting to be escorted and moving from ward to activity location as they are being actually involved in the activity. Patients have also been concerned about loss of earnings for work, owing to a reduction in the budget, and suggestions that attendance at occupational therapy should not entitle them to therapeutic earnings.

At **Broadmoor** Hospital rehabilitation trips were curtailed following two abscondions just over a year ago. The policy was subsequently clarified, so the clinical teams should now have clear reason for recommending rehabilitation trips for particular patients. The policy of strip searching all patients before trips has led to complaints from patients, who regard the practice as demeaning. At ward level, it has been unclear to what degree the policy is prescriptive or allows clinical teams' discretion, for example over the use of handcuffs.

At **Ashworth** Hospital both Commission members and the Hospital Management Group consider that rehabilitation is major area where much improvement is required. Ideally, rehabilitation provides services which prepare the patient for living outside hospital and offers 'therapy' services according to individual needs. New services are offered according to the resources available, but these are a little outdated. Commission members are currently looking at the use made by patients of off-ward area activities and the outcome and benefits of, for example, aggression management groups.

Aftercare

The establishment of adequate arrangements to identify the aftercare needs of patients leaving the Special Hospitals has received far greater priority in the last two years. There is however room for considerable future improvement.

At **Rampton** Hospital, there needs to be a much clearer policy guidance for social workers in particular in respect of assessment, planning and implementation of aftercare under Section 117 and the Care Programme Approach.

Broadmoor Hospital has had no specific Section 117 Aftercare Policy although a policy in relation to the implementation of the Care Programme Approach was introduced in 1995. In general there has been little documented preparation for discharge and there is a particular need to develop systematic assessments of patients' needs and the provision of positive rehabilitation programmes for patients.

Ashworth Hospital has recently implemented a Section 117 Aftercare Policy and Procedure.

Advocacy/Patients' Council

In its 5th Biennial Report the Commission welcomed the effort which was being put into the development of Patients' Councils and Advocacy Services following the strong recommendations in this regard in the Ashworth Inquiry Report. Initiatives have continued to be taken but overall the Commission has been disappointed with the progress made in the past two years.

In 1993 **Rampton** Hospital secured funding for an independent person to support the work of the Patients' Council for an experimental period of one year and also to consider how the advocacy needs of the patients could be addressed and to make proposals to both the Patients' Council and the Managers of the hospital. Both aims have been achieved and a proposal to establish an Advocacy Service is currently being considered. The Commission hopes that it will be possible to establish an adequately resourced Advocacy Service at the earliest possible opportunity.

The **Broadmoor** Hospital Management Team have supported the establishment of a Patients' Council which recently produced its first annual report, which is of the highest quality. Commission Members have had two meetings with the Council and anticipate further meetings at their invitation. Patients have suggested to Commission members that some members of the Council may be pursuing their own agenda rather than truly representing patients and, in addition, that many patients are not interested in "community" activity and do not participate. Commission members are aware of these difficulties (which are not unique to Patients' Councils) in trying to develop a truly representative Patients' Council and will continue to take an interest in the activities of the Council as it develops. The local CAB provides very limited advocacy services and the Commission is disappointed that no development has taken place in the last two years.

A substantial and well-funded patient Advocacy Service (Ashworth Citizens Advice Bureau Advocacy Service) has been established at **Ashworth** Hospital. Not only does it offer individual patient advocacy services but it also provides support for the Patients' Council. The Commission has admired the way in which it has established itself and the beneficial impact that it is beginning to have not only for patients but for the hospital as a whole. This service illustrates the priority given by the hospital to advocacy and the Commission hopes that a similar priority will soon be given in the other Special Hospitals.

Professional Issues

In the last two years, local difficulties in recruiting forensic psychiatrists, particularly at Rampton Hospital, trained nurses at Broadmoor Hospital, occupational therapists at Ashworth Hospital and psychologists generally have persisted. The current expansion in the number of medium secure beds is likely to exacerbate this problem. Resolution is not easy but it must continue to be accorded the highest national and local priority.

At **Broadmoor** Hospital many patients experience frequent changes of RMO, largely because of recruitment problems. This has obvious negative effects on the continuity of ongoing formulation of patients' needs and treatment plans, and the development of patients' relationships with their RMOs. The hospital's standard of a minimum contact with an RMO once every two months is commonly not being met. The Commission hears more often of nurses offering specialised treatment such as counselling. This leads Commission members to believe that the hospital could usefully employ more psychotherapists and psychologists.

The clinical notes are, in some cases, in a very poor state of order, e.g. there are no current treatment plans, muddled sections, and an absence of reports by other professionals, who keep their own files separately. One way of relieving this problem would be by the appointment of ward clerks, whose responsibility would be to ensure appropriate files are compiled with all professionals' notes and information in one place. Visiting Commission members will pay particular attention to the quality of multi-disciplinary treatment plans as a priority over the next year.

The standard of multi-disciplinary work at **Ashworth** Hospital remains a disappointment to the Commission. Some RMOs are committed to multidisciplinary working and are successfully driving this model forward. The Commission considers it unfortunate that the hospital management structure excludes the doctors in as far as the clinical manager of each of the four units manages all staff with the exception of doctors.

At **Rampton** Hospital Commission members have expressed concern about the state of the hospital's Social Work Department. The lack of leadership in setting clear objectives and priorities which can be supervised and the Department's perception that it has no adequate voice at management level has resulted in a very disjointed and patchy service to patients and their families. Of particular concern has been the impact of these deficiencies on the quality of the discussions between social workers and patients and their families about their rights under the Mental Health Act and the procedures for appeal, the tasks that need to be undertaken in preparation for Mental Health Review Tribunals and the level of understanding of issues affecting women and members of black and ethnic minority groups within the hospital. It is hoped that the appointment of a new manager will result in these problems being effectively addressed.

Review of Manager's Decisions to Withhold Patients' Mail

The Commission has a statutory duty under Section 121(7) of the Mental Health Act to review decisions by the Managers of the Special Hospitals to withhold postal packets. Outgoing mail from patients may be withheld if it is considered that the postal packet is likely to cause distress to the addressee or anyone else (other than a member of the hospital staff) or is likely to cause danger to any other person. Incoming mail can be withheld if it is thought necessary to do so in the interests of the safety of the patient or for the protection of others. Such decisions are subject to review by the Commission at the request of the patient and the Commission is entitled to order the release of the postal packet.

During the period under review, decisions to withhold incoming mail were reviewed by the Commission on three occasions at Ashworth hospital, on three occasions at Broadmoor hospital but on no occasions at Rampton hospital.

Access To Telephones

When the Mental Health Act was being considered by Parliament, patient access to telephones in the Special Hospitals was unknown and, as a consequence, the Act contains no regulations governing the supervision or restriction of such access in the way that the Act contains important provisions about postal packets and their withholding.

The Commission has warmly welcomed the introduction of access to telephones for patients. It recognises that such access has to be supervised and it has strongly supported the production of policies and procedures that are clearly understood by both patients and staff.

Mail addressed to a number of organisations listed in Section 134 of the Act (the Commission is one) cannot be withheld by the Managers of the Special Hospitals. The Commission holds the view that patient telephone calls to the same organisations should attract a similar degree of privacy and that whilst any supervision of phone calls should not generally include listening into the contents of the calls (in certain circumstances this may be necessary) such listening in should never take place when the patient's phone call is with one of the specific organisations referred to above.

A lack of understanding of the current policy and procedures by staff together with technical limitations in some of the Special Hospital telephone systems makes this difficult to achieve and the highest priority must be attached to rectifying this position.

Patients with Learning Disabilities in Special Hospitals

The number of patients with learning disabilities in the Special Hospitals has, appropriately, considerably declined over the past few years and the SHSA is to be congratulated on this achievement. The Commission remains aware, however, that a significant number of patients with learning disability remain. Most are in Rampton Hospital with a number still in Ashworth Hospital and a very small number in Broadmoor Hospital.

Members of the Commission have seen the Special Hospital Service Authority's strategy and policy statement for patients with learning disability. The policy envisages a "super specialty" service within the high security service to provide care and treatment for a difficult group of patients. The Board has decided that Rampton Hospital should be the principal focus for the proposed service and the sole location for future admission of patients with a principal diagnosis of learning disability. It has also proposed that Ashworth Hospital should continue to provide an in-patient service for its residual learning disabilities population but should not admit new patients to that service. It appears that patients with "secondary learning disabilities diagnosis" will be admitted to Ashworth Hospital in the future and also to Broadmoor Hospital.

The Commission considers that provision of services for people who require a high degree of security should be based on a locally accessible service to enable patients to remain in contact with families, carers and other local services. The Commission have long been aware of problems in discharging patients who have spent long periods of time in conditions of high security in Special Hospitals which are isolated and have had weak links with local rehabilitation services. The proposed SHSA policy will not change this and will concentrate provision for a particularly difficult group of patients on one site in Nottinghamshire. The Commission has serious concerns about this proposal. Additional concerns about secure provision include;

- Provision of local secure care and rehabilitation to patients
- Continuing delays in transferring those patients who are presently in Special Hospitals and do not need high security
- The provision of appropriate mental health care for patients in secure hospitals and the community who have both a learning disability and a mental health problem.

Section IV

Priorities in Community Care

10 *Community Care*

10.1 Introduction

During the second year of the biennial review period public attention has been focused sharply on the quality and effectiveness of Community Care, notably following the publication of the reports of the inquiries into the treatment and care of Christopher Clunis, Andrew Robinson and John Rous.

The Commission's statutory interest in Community Care relates primarily to the work of Approved Social Workers (ASWs) and the operation of Section 117 of the Mental Health Act, but in their regular visits to NHS Trusts and Social Services Departments, members of the Commission have increasingly faced the whole range of issues concerning the care and management of patients in the community who were formerly detained in hospital. The effectiveness of this aftercare has great significance for patients, patient organisations and for carers, who see it as a fundamental issue influencing the likelihood of readmission.

The ready availability of supportive services and the quality of supervision provided to patients in care and following discharge are also widely regarded as key factors in the management of risk for patients, carers and the general public.

The enquiries referred to above have involved homicides, an outcome which the Commission regards with the greatest concern. The Commission is also mindful that the Health of the Nation targets have highlighted the significant risks of suicides for people who suffer from enduring mental illnesses. For example this accounts for 10% of the deaths of patients who suffer from schizophrenia. The Commission hopes that publicity attending the continuing run of inquiry reports will also make mention of these issues, so that a broader and better informed popular perspective may be encouraged.

The Commission has given attention to the implications for detained patients of the NHS and Community Care Act 1990, implemented in April 1993. Particular consideration has been given to the impact of relevant sections in relation to the Code of Practice and on the implementation of Section 117 of the Mental Health Act. Also identified with these issues are the effects of changes in legislation relating to Income Maintenance and Welfare benefits for severely mentally ill people detained in hospital. Between them these revisions to legislation have very significant consequences for the rehabilitation and the aftercare arrangements for patients, particularly those who are the most disabled and dependant as a result of mental disorder.

10.2 Section 117 and the Care Programme Approach

Since 1991, Health Authorities and local authorities have been expected to introduce procedures for the Care Programme Approach and Care Management Approach, respectively. RMOs and ASWs are key players in the successful implementation of Section 117 and the Care Programme Approach. However, although in many areas joint procedures have been put in place, the commitment to using them by operational staff in some localities remains a problem.

However many Commission reports record improved practice in relation to Section 117, in that meetings are taking place. Families, patients and participants in the aftercare process are more frequently invited to attend meetings on discharge and care planning.

Problems still reported include;
- Poor recording of care plans, particularly unmet needs
- Meetings being arranged at the last minute
- Difficulties in arranging Section 117 meetings prior to discharge
- No flagging of reviews of Section 117 meetings
- A scarcity and lack of variety in the range of services in the community. The principles of Community Care have in many places not been easy to achieve because of restrictions imposed by lack of resources.

10.3 Supervision Registers and Supervised Discharge

New guidelines issued by the Secretary of State for Health required Health Authorities to ensure that all mental health service provider units introduce Supervision Registers by 1st October 1994 of persons known to be at serious risk to themselves or to others. This provision does not apply in Wales.

As part of their visits to hospitals, Commission members are in a position to monitor the implementation of the registers as they relate to patients detained under the Act. Most, if not all, provider units have now set up registers but the Commission has concerns about implementation in some instances.

The three criteria for inclusion on the register are:

- significant risk of suicide
- significant risk of serious violence to others
- significant risk of severe self-neglect.

The Commission is concerned to ensure that:

- criteria for inclusion on the register are adhered to
- regular reviews take place
- information about their inclusion on a register is freely available to patients
- evidence demonstrating that a patient should be included on the register is recorded in writing
- there is liaison with GPs and the local Social Services Department
- there are sound reasons for not advising a patient of their inclusion on the register.

Implementation of Supervision Registers

Since the introduction of the registers, members of the Commission have discussed on their visits to Trusts their implementation as they relate to detained patients. In addition to the Departmental guidance, the Commission has issued guidance to its own members emphasising, in particular, the importance of setting the registers against the broader framework of the Care Programme Approach.

Members of the Commission have been informed on visits to some hospitals that although "token" Supervision Registers have been produced, they are not being fully implemented.

Initial implementation of the registers has thrown up problems of interpretation of the guidance relating to inclusion on the register, to informing the patient of inclusion and concerning access to the registers. These are all areas in which Commission members have noted a wide variation in practice. Further guidance from the Department of Health is required to resolve these anomalies.

For example, members on one visit found that a criterion for inclusion appeared to be that an individual was thought to have committed a crime, and on another it was discovered that the local policy provided for the police to be notified of everybody placed on the register. On a number of occasions, a lack of understanding amongst professional groups not employed by the Health Service, including Approved Social Workers, as to how they relate to the registers has been apparent. However, despite such examples the general perception of Commission members is that a great deal of time and effort has been devoted to attempting to ensure that the registers are properly implemented. In circumstances where the relevant parties have conflicting interests, these are properly taken into account. The Department of Health has informed the Commission that it has commissioned comprehensive research into how the registers are being used and how effective they are perceived to be. The Commission will await the outcome of this study with interest.

There is discussion of the Supervision Register in relation to mentally disordered offenders in Chapter 7.4.

10.4   Movement of Patients into the Community

The creation of NHS Trusts has brought marked changes in the delivery of care to people with mental illness. In many places, hospital units have closed or the in-patient provision has been reduced. In most cases this has been accompanied by an increase in community provision of psychiatric services and social support, mainly by the development of interdisciplinary Community Mental Health Teams and increased provision of supported community residential facilities. In general this has led to a significant improvement in the standard and level of Community Care. However, the most serious repercussions on in-patient care, which have resulted from reducing hospital provision in the absence of adequate or sufficient community support, are being felt most heavily in acute admission wards.

Whilst many long-stay and elderly mentally ill patients have been successfully relocated into community settings, there remains a core of patients who are unable to make the transition and for whom Community Care is arguably the least preferred option. This reality can become lost in the pressure for, and process of, change in each locality.

For many people with enduring mental illness/severe mental illness the acute ward environment is disturbing, which in turn results in increased ward management and nursing problems. Long term rehabilitation and resettlement cannot easily be achieved within the confines of present day acute wards with high bed occupancy rates, high percentages of detained patients and increasing numbers of patients manifesting difficult to manage behaviour. As a result many units have a significant proportion of patients staying in hospital as long as 6 months and often over 12 months, all awaiting transfer to the community, delayed by lack of access to rehabilitation units or supported accommodation.

For some patients undergoing rehabilitation, return to the community is prematurely enforced by the need to discharge in order to free up beds. The result of such unplanned discharge is often early return into hospital and the creation of a "revolving door" situation.

In 1991 The Department of Health suggested that service planners should give consideration to the provision of 24 hour staffed care homes in the community, with care provided by nurses with no doctors resident on site. The objective was to create suitable community alternatives to long-stay hospital care for people with long-term mental illness who require this level of support. The Department has identified that the provision of such community facilities is very slow and has asked the Mental Health Act Commission to raise this issue in their discussions with Health Commissioning Agencies and Trusts.

10.5 Problems in Residential Care from Out-of-area Placements

In some parts of the country, the Commission has received reports from Trusts of an increasing placement of vulnerable people from elsewhere in the country into residential care in their catchment areas. These out of district placements can have a significant impact on the services available to local populations. Such residents are often placed in accommodation such as private bed and breakfast establishments, small hotels and non-registered multi-occupancy dwellings let mainly to DSS clients. Often they are placed by distant local authorities or Trusts without planned discharge or appropriate follow-up arrangements, or with very limited follow-up lasting for only a few weeks. Their presence is not detected until they again become unwell. Such factors may to contribute the high bed occupancy rates in some areas.

It is said that many of these patients originate from London Boroughs or from Liverpool.

There is a clear need for better arrangements for placing, providing care for and funding both health and social needs of such vulnerable people far from their homes or referring areas. A comprehensive research study is to be undertaken by the University of Kent.

10.6   Community Support Teams

The work of Community Support Teams is often slow, arduous and repetitive with relatively static groups of patients, many of whom have been part of the "revolving door" syndrome. The information produced by such teams indicates that many of the long-stay patients from the past have become long-term clients in the community and very few will be re-admitted into the hospital system. The evidence from users, carers and professionals indicates that, in general, aftercare systems have helped prevent patients from relapsing and that further expansion of such adequately resourced schemes is required.

10.7   Approved Social Workers

Members of the Commission continue to express their satisfaction with the developing role of Approved Social Workers (ASWs) and their ability to handle effectively the often complex elements involved in Community Care of psychiatric patients. These skills are, however, very task-specific and will need to be developed further, as the recently published statement of Competencies for Forensic Social Work has shown. (Central Council for Education and Training in Social Work 1995)

Approved Social Workers in a Time of Change

The Commission views Approved Social Workers as central to the delivery of local authority services to people with mental health problems and in particular, those with severe and enduring mental illness.

In the purchaser-provider split, the Commission believes that the role of the Approved Social Worker should be much wider than processing compulsory admissions. In addition they need to;

- have a sufficient knowledge of mental health resources to meet the requirement of section 13 of the Act and be able to seek the least restrictive alternative
- understand the roles and responsibilities of other mental health professionals and develop a positive working relationship with them
- provide continuity of service where possible and have some knowledge of the different stages of a person's mental distress

Reports from Commission visits indicate that, where ASWs act as Care Managers and have adequate control over resources, they are more effectively empowered to search for the least restrictive alternative. In addition, in some areas they are able to remain in contact with the client and this is seen to be desirable. However, practice varies considerably and there have been problems identified in some areas. A common complaint from patients is that they never see the same Approved Social Worker twice. Commission members frequently receive comments from users, carers and professionals which indicate that continuity of ASW involvement is beneficial.

Approved Social Workers often comment that the implementation of care management has created increased administrative tasks, particularly form filling. This is especially true within mental health because of the separate documentation required for the different monitoring and reviewing systems(Care Management, the Care Programme Approach and the requirements of Section 117).

Approved Social Workers often find themselves in a service brokerage role, commissioning work to be performed by other individuals or agencies, which in the past would have been undertaken by themselves. Whilst this work is accepted as an appropriate and necessary use of their skills, they feel that the relationship and counselling skills resulting from their training and experience are not being effectively utilised and that these tasks are increasingly being undertaken by less skilled, qualified and experienced staff.

Another major concern which has been expressed to the Commission is that the introduction of Supervision Registers and the prospect of supervised after-care arrangements, which may threaten the independence of social workers because of the greater responsibility and accountability which is placed on the Responsible Medical Officer by these provisions.

ASWs have reported favourably on the quality of their in-service refresher training. This has often been innovative, has responded to their training needs and appears to have evolved through the initiatives of training officers. Much of the training has been practice-based and there has also been an increase in training in most pertinent areas, such as forensic psychiatry.

Concerns continue to be expressed about the safety of ASWs and the professional support which they receive, especially out of normal office hours. Where emergency services are provided on an agency basis, ASWs are having to manage crises on unfamiliar ground and may not be familiar with local resources which could be used as an alternative to admission.

Continuing gaps in out-of-hours provision are still widely reported, and comprehensive multi-disciplinary crisis intervention services are still a rarity. In many localities, services are not provided as an extension of specialised day time mental health services, but by staff from other sectors of social services who have retained their ASW accreditation, whilst working primarily with, for example children, families or disabled people. The Commission continues to be concerned over the briefing and follow up responsibilities of such workers who are located out of the mainstream of mental health work.

ASWs continue to express generalised concerns about the lack of provision for services as a genuine alternative to hospital admission.

Approved Social Workers' Experience of Change

During 1994/1995 the Commission examined this topic by giving questionnaires to each group of ASWs visited during a 6 month period from 01/03/94 to 31/08/94.

Their responses indicated that:

- The purchaser/provider divide of Local Authorities and SSDs has led to difficulties for ASWs. Clearly there is a lack of equity in decision making, i.e. in some authorities the ASW is purchaser, in others a provider and in a few the ASW straddles between.

- The legislation has forced ASWs to be bound up with assessment. Completion of standardised assessment procedures has forced them into the role of care managers, spending much of their time completing forms and acting as mediator for patients, carers and other concerned professionals.

- Many ASWs report that their present role and function in relation to mental health is often predominantly linked with their statutory duties under the Mental Health Act. Prevention and aftercare in these circumstances tends to be relegated to second place.

10.8 Mental Illness Specific Grant

The welcomed proposal by the Department of Health to establish a Mental Illness Specific Grant available to local authorities was implemented in 1991 and was planned to run for 3 years. Local authorities were encouraged to propose innovatory schemes for the care of mentally ill people residing in the community and 70% of the cost could be claimed back from the Department of Health with the balance to be met locally. Virtually all local authorities applied for the grant by putting forward a wide range of proposals, the majority of which were successful. Not all the proposals demonstrated an original approach to aspects of community care, as some local authorities perceived the grant as a way of subsidising existing services. On the whole, however, the MISG has succeeded in establishing a range of new and additional services relating to sections of the population who had often been missed by existing provision.

The MISG was planned to terminate at the end of the 1993/1994 financial year much to the disappointment of these local authorities which had not made provision to continue with services subsidised by the grant. The resulting insecurity and anxiety evident at that time amongst employees who had specialised knowledge and experience was noted by Commission members. Late in the day, the Specific Grant was renewed but only for a further limited period. It is important that local authorities reach firm decisions whether or not to maintain future services established under the provisions of the Mental Illness Specific Grant. The Commission supports the continuation of some similar grant process, but the emphasis should remain on the introduction of new additional provisions and should require local authorities to make application detailing the nature and purpose of any proposed service development for longer term mentally ill persons living in the community. It should not be used to subsidise currently existing services.

10.9 Income Maintenance and Welfare Benefits Issues

Income Maintenance and Welfare Benefits Issues

An essential element of any Care Programme, and of successful after-care, is ensuring that patients receive their full entitlement to social security benefits. However, over the past two years there is increasing evidence arising both from visits to hospitals and Social Services Departments, and from complaints to the Commission, that these issues are causing serious disadvantage to detained patients, both during their stay in hospital and at the point of discharge.

The social security regulations affect hospital patients in a particularly complex way. Disability Living Allowance (care component) ceases after four weeks in hospital; incapacity benefit is downrated by approximately 30% after six weeks, and income support is reduced to a weekly hospital pocket-money rate (currently £14.70), after the same period. Where patients are receiving incapacity benefit and housing benefit for accommodation in the community, their personal liability for rent increases after six weeks in hospital, an aspect of the regulations that is very little understood. Communication with the Benefits Agency and the local authority is essential to ensure that patients receive the correct level of benefits, but many detained patients are too ill to attend to these matters for themselves.

The Commission has been alerted to cases where serious indebtedness has resulted from the impact of these regulations combined with a lack of communication between the agencies involved. It is clearly essential in these circumstances that all agencies involved in this process (the hospital, the Benefits Agency, the housing authority and the patient's key worker) should work closely together to ensure that the right benefits are paid at the right time. The Commission considers that responsibility for ensuring income maintenance should be written into every patient's Care Programme.

Eligibility for Community Care Grants

Community Care Grants are intended to help people on Income Support who are "facing difficulty arising from special circumstances and in particular to support the policy of Care in the Community". Their purpose is to help certain priority groups, including mentally ill people, to re-establish themselves or remain in the community .

However, some patients, because of their contribution record while employed, receive Incapacity (previously Invalidity) Benefit rather than Income Support. This precludes them from being able to claim a community care grant, as only those in receipt of Income Support are eligible to apply for this discretionary benefit. The result is that for some patients, ready for discharge, offers of accommodation are jeopardised as they have few if any resources with which to set up home. Circumstances of this kind add to the difficulties of effective discharge planning under Section 117.

Information, Advice and Advocacy

Given the complexity of the benefits system, particularly as it applies to hospital patients, the availability of information, advice and advocacy in income maintenance and welfare benefits is of the utmost importance for detained patients.

The Commission welcomes the growth in the provision of such services. A number of voluntary organisations, particularly the National Association of Citizens Advice Bureaux and MIND, are increasingly taking their services into hospitals. Nevertheless, the majority of hospitals still lack this sort of provision, and where it exists it is often under-resourced. The Commission considers that the provision of a skilled and properly funded advocacy service should be an essential element of the hospital care of detained patients, and that purchasers should include it in every contract for the provision of such care.

10.10   General Practitioners

The Commission remains aware that there are deficiencies in some GPs' knowledge of the Mental Health Act and that only a small percentage of GPs are Section 12 Approved Doctors.

Notably there are criticisms of some GPs' medical recommendations in support of applications for patients to be detained, particularly where insufficient reason is given why informal admission or other methods of care or treatment would not be appropriate. In general the simple statement of a diagnosis does not constitute an adequate medical recommendation.

More use could be made of Section 15(2) of the Act which allows Hospital Managers to ask for a fresh medical recommendation complying with the relevant provisions of Part 1 of the Act, within 14 days of the hospital admission.

For most GPs, a compulsory admission of their patients under the Mental Health Act is an infrequent procedure (less than once every two years on average), so they are not on familiar ground when making a recommendation for a patient to be detained. Most will look to their consultant psychiatrist colleagues for guidance on these occasions.

Post graduate training in the Mental Health Act does not have a high priority for most GPs. Under their contracts, they may claim a specific payment (Postgraduate Education Allowance) if they attend on average 5 days of post graduate training a year on a five year rolling programme. The choice of subjects, within broad categories, is at the discretion of the GP. Most concentrate on disease management, new developments in medicine and practice management.

The Commission continues to give consideration to methods of increasing GPs' awareness and knowledge of the Mental Health Act and is exploring three mechanisms, namely, continuing education via GP tutors at post graduate medical centres, articles in medical journals and publications read by GPs, and the development of a Mental Health Act Commission practice note. (A Commission briefing note has been prepared and will be ready in the near future for direct circulation to all GPs).

Section V

11 The Commission in Wales

The Effect of New Laws on the Commission's Work

Over the last four years there has been a marked change in the structure of the National Health Service in the wake of the split between purchasing and provider services, and also a marked increase in the number of NHS Trusts. Between July 1993 and June 1995 the Commission twice visited the mental health services of nine NHS Trusts in seven of the eight counties in Wales.

After the NHS and Community Care Act, 1990, local authorities were given greater resources and greater responsibilities for the provision of community services, including services for the mentally ill. In some counties in Wales, the Commission has heard of the beneficial effects of the Act on community services for people suffering from mental illness; in one county, however, lack of suitable community provision by the local authority still appeared to be impeding the transfer of patients from hospital.

The Welsh Language Act 1993 requires that public bodies which provide services to the public in Wales should prepare a Welsh language scheme, and it is likely that the Welsh Office will include the Mental Health Act Commission in the list of such bodies. The Commission fully recognises the importance of the Welsh language in the execution of its work in Wales, and is giving careful consideration to this requirement.

In April 1996 local authority boundaries will change in that the present counties of Wales will disappear to be replaced by a number of Unitary Authorities. At the same time the number of District Health Authorities will be reduced. With respect to mental health services, this entails re-establishing the good understanding and working relationships between community and health services which are so important for creating a good overall service. The Commission trusts that these substantial changes will not slow down the complete implementation of the Mental Health Plans of the present counties of Wales. In many respects, the observations made below mirror those reported in England.

Visits

The Commission carried out 33 visits during the period 1st July 1993-30th June 1995, which included 26 psychiatric hospitals, 5 hospitals for learning disability, 2 forensic units, and the 8 Social Services Departments in the 8 counties of Wales.

As far as possible, the Commission Visiting Team for Wales tries to arrange joint visits between health services (Trusts and units directly managed by Health Authorities) and Social Services Departments. In this way a more comprehensive picture is obtained of the operation of the Mental Health Act, which includes the procedures of compulsory admission, care and treatment in hospital, and aftercare.

On the whole, joint visits have proved very worthwhile, but following the increase in the number of NHS Trusts, some problems have arisen in arranging joint visits with the county SSDs, particularly in those counties in which more than one Trust provides mental health services. The Commission is confident, however, that with goodwill, these problems, and any others that may arise following the county boundary changes in April 1996, can be overcome.

The Commission visits one Registered Mental Nursing Home, Llanarth Court Hospital, which is run by a private company and admits patients detained under the Mental Health Act. It is likely that other similar nursing homes, taking detained patients, will be established in Wales over the next few years and will be visited by the Commission.

In the future, the Commission intends to arrange visits to purchasers as well as the providers of mental health services.

Changes in the Mental Health Services

The Commission's Fifth Biennial Report referred to the changing pattern of services for people with mental health problems, based upon a move away from treatment in large psychiatric hospitals to more accessible and acceptable community-based services. This process continues with the closure of Park Hospital in Mid Glamorgan in 1994, and the ongoing closure of North Wales Hospital in Clwyd.

The provision of local, easily accessible services is generally welcomed by the Commission as is the intention to strengthen community services and reduce the need for admission to hospital. The Commission has received appreciative reports of the work of Community Mental Health Teams in many areas. There are examples of effective and praiseworthy co-operation between NHS services, the community services of the local authorities, the voluntary services, and the private sector. During visits in Wales, the general impression is of good services provided by dedicated workers, who are well trained in the care of the mentally ill and in the requirements of the Mental Health Act. There are, however, some concerns expressed by the Commission about the implementation of these changes.

Some Anxieties about the Changes

Of the various anxieties about the changes in the provision of mental health services, the following are mentioned since they are especially relevant to people who are admitted compulsorily to hospitals under the Mental Health Act.

- A substantial number of the inhabitants of some counties (e.g. Pembrokeshire, Dyfed, Gwynedd and Powys) live a considerable distance from acute hospital services. There are, however, plans in a number of these counties to develop additional acute services when resources become available, which the Commission welcomes.

- The shortage of beds in acute psychiatric services in some areas leads to pressure on existing beds and an unsuitable mix of patients. The Commission is concerned that the number of beds created by the new acute units will be insufficient to rectify this situation. Whilst the Commission supports the intention to develop good community services, it is concerned that this should not be to the detriment of acute hospital services.

- There is a lack of provision for people with serious, long-term mental illnesses as traditional mental hospitals are being run down and closed. As was noted in the Fifth Report, special attention still needs to be given to making adequate provision for this comparatively small group. Members of the Commission continue to meet such people who have to accept care on acute wards and in forensic units because of want of proper provision for them.

- In all parts of Wales there is a need to develop and strengthen community services; to increase the number of community mental health teams, day hospitals, and homes that provide a proper level of care for people with long-term mental health problems of all degrees of severity.

An Increase in Forensic Services

During this Biennial Report period Caswell Clinic, a Medium Secure Unit in Mid Glamorgan, has been extended to take 33 patients. Llanarth Court Hospital in Gwent, a Registered Mental Nursing Home, has also opened an additional ward, and now provides around 60 beds. The plan to establish a Medium Secure Unit on the site of Bryn y Neuadd Hospital in East Gwynedd was delayed by the requirement to go out to private tender.

The Commission visits each forensic unit twice a year, and with the increasing number of patients in these units in Wales, the Commission is under an increasing obligation to provide more resources for these visits.

The Operation of the Mental Health Act 1983

The completion and checking of the legal documents pertaining to the Mental Health Act by records officers and by psychiatrists is of a high standard, and any necessary corrections are carried out within the authorised time.

Very few incorrect documents (which can make a patient's compulsory detention illegal) are found by Commission members during their visits.

Despite this, there are some problems, especially with regard to Part IV of the Act, which deals with consent to treatment. The most important is the failure in some cases to ensure that the type or level of medication given to the patient is within that authorised on Form 38 or 39. It is mainly the responsibility of psychiatrists and also of nurses who administer medication, to ensure that the medication given is lawful. Not infrequently, there is also a failure to complete Form 38 according to the recommendations of the Act's Code of Practice. The Commission stresses the importance of applying this part of the Act correctly.

Problems in Assessing the Need for Compulsory Admission to Hospital

Coming to a decision about the need for compulsory admission to hospital is difficult and distressing for the person concerned and his/her family. Apart from the assessment of the family doctor, the assessment of two other persons is usually required, that of another doctor approved as having "special experience in the diagnosis or treatment of mental disorder" (Section 12(2) of the Mental Health Act), and that of an Approved Social Worker (Section 114). Indeed, in most cases if a decision is taken to make an application for compulsory admission this doctor and an Approved Social Worker have to sign two of the legal documents that are necessary for admission.

However, in some counties, there are problems in providing the services of Approved Social Workers out of hours and at week-ends. A county-wide emergency team is often responsible for services at such times, but there can be difficulties because of the long distance sometimes involved. In one county for over a year no Approved Social Worker services at all were provided during night-time hours, and this often causes great difficulties for the patient, his family, the family doctor and the police. It is the responsibility of local authorities to provide a 24 hour service to meet the sometimes urgent requirements of the Mental Health Act.

There is a shortage of doctors approved under Section 12(2) of the Act in many counties. Sometimes, it seems likely that this is the main reason for the large number of admissions under Section 4 of the Act, which allows admissions with only one medical recommendation instead of the customary two. However, the purpose of Section 4 is to allow emergency admission, when having to wait a few hours for the opinion of a doctor approved under Section 12(2) is judged to carry an unacceptable risk. It is a misuse of Section 4 to use it because a Section 12(2) doctor, as was reported in one instance, is not available for three days.

The District Health Authority has the responsibility of ensuring that there is a sufficient number of Section 12 doctors, and that an up-to-date list is available for social workers. The Commission stresses the importance of an assessment and recommendation by a doctor with experience in the field of mental illness when the social worker makes a decision about an application for compulsory admission.

12 Y Comisiwn Yng Nghymru

Effaith Cyfreithiau Newydd ar waith y Comisiwn

Yn ystod y pedair blynedd diwethaf bu cryn newid yn strwythur y Gwasanaeth Iechyd Cenedlaethol (GIC) yn sgil y toriad rhwng gwasanaethau prynu a gwasanaethau darpar, a bu cynnydd mawr yn nifer yr Ymddiriedolaethau GIC. Rhwng Gorffenaf 1993 a Mehefin 1995, bu'r Comisiwn yn ymweld ddwyaith â gwasanaethau iechyd meddwl naw o Ymddiriedolaethau, yn saith o wyth sir Cymru.

Wedi Deddf GIC a Gofal Cymunedol 1990, rhoddwyd mwy o adnoddau i awdurdodau lleol, a mwy o gyfrifoldeb arnynt i ddarpar gwasanaethau cymunedol, gan gynnwys gwasanaethau ar gypher pobl â phroblemau iechyd meddwl. Yn ystod ei ymweliadau, clywodd y Comisiwn an effaith llesol hyn ar ofal pobl ag anabledd oherwydd afiechyd meddwl yn rhai siroedd, ond yn un sir, dywedwyd fod diffyg darpar gwasanaethau cymunedol gan y llywodraeth leol o hyd yn oedi trosglwyddo pobl ag anabledd o'r ysbyty i'r gymuned.

Y mae Deddf yr Iaith Gymraeg, 1993, yn gofyn am gynllun iaith Gymraeg gan gyrff cyhoeddus sy'n darpar gwasanaethau i'r cyhoedd yng Nghymru, ac y mae'n debyg y bydd y Swyddfa Gymreig yn cynnwys Comisiwn y Ddeddf Iechyd Meddwl yn y rhestr o'r cyrff hyn. Y mae'r Comisiwn yn llawn gydnabod pwysigrwydd yr iaith wrth gyflawni ei waith yng Nghymru, ac yn trafod y gofynion hyn ar hyn o bryd.

Yn Ebrill 1996, bwriedir dileu'r siroedd presennol, a chreu nifer o awdurdodau newydd, yr Awdurdodau Unedol. Ar yr un pryd, bwriedir lleihau nifer yr Awdurdodau Iechyd Dosbarth yng Nghymru. O safbwynt gwasanaethau iechyd meddwl, golyga hyn y bydd yn rhaid ail-greu, i raddau beth bynnag, y cyd-ddealltwriaeth a'r cydweithrediad rhwng gwasanaethau cymunedol a'r gwasanaethau iechyd sydd mor bwysig i wasanaeth da cyflawn. Rhaid sefydlu perthynas newydd, hefyd, rhwng yr Ymddiriedolaethau a'r Awdurdodau Prynu. Y mae'r Comisiwn yn hyderu na fydd y newidiadau sylweddol hyn yn oedi cyflawniad Cynlluniau Iechyd Meddwl siroedd presennol Cymru.

I raddau helaeth, y mae'r sylwadau a wneir isod yn berthnasol hefyd i Loegr.

Ymweliadau

Gwnaeth y Comisiwn 33 o ymweliadau rhwng Gorffennaf 1993 a Mehefin 1995, ac yn ystod y rhain ymwelodd â 26 o ysbytai seiciatrig, 5 ysbyty anabledd dysgu, 2 uned fforensig, ac 8 Adran Gwasanaethau Cymdeithasol.

Ceisodd Tîm Ymweled y Comisiwn dros Gymru i drefnu ymweliadau ar y cyd rhwng awdurdodau iechyd darpar (Ymddiriedolaethau a rhai Awdurdodau Iechyd) ac AGC y siroedd. Wrth wneud hyn, ceir darlun cyflawnach o'r modd y gweithredir y Ddeddf Iechyd Meddwl, o drefniadaethau derbyniad gorfodol, gofal a thriniaeth ysbyty, ac unrhyw ddarpariaethau ar gyfer gofal a thriniaeth bellach yn y gymuned wedyn.

Ar y cyfan bu ymweliadau ar y cyd yn foddhaol iawn, ond gyda'r cynnydd yn nifer yr Ymddiriedolaethau, cododd rhai anawsterau wrth geisio trefnu ymweliadau ar y cyd ag AGC y siroedd, yn enwedig yn y siroedd hynny lle mae mwy nag un Ymddiririedolaeth yn darpar gwasanaethau iechyd meddwl. Gydag ewyllys da, beth bynnag, mae'r Comisiwn yn ffyddiog y gellir datrys y problemau hyn, gan gynnwys y rhai a all ddod o newidiadau Ebrill, 1996.

Y mae'r Comisiwn yn ymweld ag un cartref iechyd meddwl sydd yn yr adran breifat, sef Ysbyty Llys Llanarth, sy'n derbyn cleifon o dan y Ddeddf Iechyd Meddwl; y tebygrwydd yw y sefydlir cartrefi eraill tebyg gan yr adran breifat yng Nghymru yn ystod y blynyddoedd nesaf.

Yn ystod y flwyddyn neu ddwy nesaf mae'r Comisiwn yn bwriadu trefnu ymweliadau hefyd â phrynwyr gwasanaethau iechyd meddwl.

Y Newidiadau yn y Gwasanaethau Iechyd Meddwl

Ym Mhumed Adroddiad y Comisiwn, soniwyd am y newidiadau dirfawr sy'n cymryd lle yn y gwasanaethau ar gyfer pobl â phroblemau iechyd meddwl. Y mae'r newidiadau hyn yn parhau, e.e. caewyd ysbyty Parc, ym Morgannwg Ganol, yn 1994, ac y mae Ysbyty Gogledd Cymru i'w gau yn y dyfodol agos.

Y mae'r bwriad i ddarpar gwasanaethau lleol, hawd eu cyrraed, yn derbyn croeso cyffredinol, fel y mae'r amcan i gryfhau gwasanaethau cymunedol, a lleihau'r gofyn am fynediad i ysbyty. Y mae'r Comisiwn wedi sylwi fel y mae gwaith y Tîmau Iechyd Meddwl Cymunedol, er enghraifft, yn cael ei werthfawrogi mewn llawer ardal. Ar y cyfan, hefyd, gwelir cydweithrediad cymeradwy rhwng gwasanaethau iechyd y GIC, gwasanaethau cymunedol llywodraethau lleol, y mudiaidau gwirfoddol, a'r sector breifat. Yr argraff a geir mewn ymweliadau dros Gymru yw o wasanaethau da gan weithwyr ymroddedig, sydd wedi eu hyffordi'n drwyadl yng ngofal y claf, ac yng ngofynion y Ddeddf Iechyd Meddwl.

Rhai Pryderon ynglŷn â'r Newidiadau.

Fel y sylwyd yn y Pumed Adroddiad, y mae rhai pryderon. Crybwyllir y rhai canlnol am eu bod yn arbennig o berthnasol i bobl sy'n cael eu derbyn i ysbytai o dan y Ddeddf Iechyd Meddwl.

- Y mae nifer sylweddol o drigolion rhai sioedd e.e. Dyfed, Gwynedd, a Phowys, yn byw ymhell o wasanaethau iechyd meddwl llym ysbytai. Y mae'r Comisiwn yn cefnogi'r bwriad i ddatblygu unedau llym ychwanegol er mwyn darpar gwasanaethau mwy cyrraeddadwy pan fydd adnoddau ar gael.

- Yn rhai ardaloedd sylwodd y Comisiwn ar brysurdeb yr unedau llym, y pwysedd arnynt, a'r cymysgedd anaddas o gleifion. Hefyd y mae peth pryder y bydd nifer y gwelyau a gynllunir ar gyfer unedau llym newydd yn annigonol. Er fod y Comisiwn yn cefnogi'r bwriad i ddatblygu gwasanaethau yn y gymuned, ni ddylid gwneud hyn ar draul sicrhau gwasanaethau digonol yn yr ysbytai.

- Y mae diffyg darpariaeth ar gyfer pobl ag afiechydon meddwl enbyd, tymor hir, wrth wacáu a chau'r ysbytai traddodiadol. Fel y dywedwyd yn Pumed Adroddiad, dylid rhoi sylw arbennig i ddarpariaeth ddigonol ar gyfer y grŵp cymharol fychan hwn. Y mae Comisiynwyr yn parhau i ddod ar draws aelodau ohono sy'n gorfod derbyn gofal ar wardiau llym ac yn unedau fforensig oherwydd diffyg darpariaeth addas ar eu cyfer.

- Ym mhob rhan o Gymru y mae galw am ddatblygu a chryfhau gwasanaethau iechyd meddwl cymunedol e.e. nifer a chryfder y tîmau cymunedol, nifer yr ysbytai dydd, a nifer y cartrefi sy'n darpar gofal addas i bobl â phroblemau tymor hir o bob gradd o enbydrwydd.

Cynnydd yn y Gwasanaethau Fforensig

Y mae'r uned diogelwch canolig, Clinig Caswell, ym Morgannwg Ganol, yn cael ei ehangu i dderbyn 33 o gleifion. Hefyd, y mae Llys Llanarth yng Ngwent, cartref nyrsio seiciatrig diogel, wedi agor ward ychwanegol, ac yn awr yn darpar cyfanswm o ryw 60 o welyau. Ar y llaw arall, y mae'r cynllun i sefydlu uned diogelwch canolig ar safle Ysbyty Bryn y Neuadd yn nwyrain Gwynedd wedi ei ohirio, oherwydd y gofyn i geisio tendrau o'r sector breifat.

Y mae'r Comisiwn yn ymweld â phob uned fforensig ddwywaith y flwyddyn a gyda'r cynnydd yn nifer y cleifion yn yr unedau hyn yng Nghymru, y mae o dan rwymedigaeth cynyddol i ddarpar mwy o adnoddau ar gyfer yr ymweliadau hyn.

Gweithrediad Deddf Iechyd Meddwl, 1983.

Y mae'r archwiliad o'r dogfennau cyfreithlon sy'n perthyn i'r Ddeddf gan swyddogion cofnodion yr ysbytai a gan seiciatryddion, o safon uchel, ac unrhyw gywiriadau cyfreithlon a fydd eisiau, yn cael eu gwneud o fewn yr amser awdurdodedig. Ychydig iawn o ddogfennau anghywir (a all wneud derbyniad gorfodol y claf yn anghyfreithlon) a ddarganfyddir gan Gomisiynwyr ar eu hymweliadau.

Serch hyn, y mae rhai problemau, yn enwedig ynglŷn â gweithrediad Rhan 4 o'r Ddeddf, sy'n ymwneud â chantiatâd i driniaeth. Y pwysicaf yw'r diffyg, mewn ambell achos, i sicrhau fod math a lefel y feddginiaeth a roir i'r claf o fewn y terfynau a awdurdodir ar ffurflenni 38 a 39. Cyfrifoldeb y seiciatryddion yn bennaf, ond hefyd y nyrsys sy'n rhoi'r feddyginiaeth, yw sicrhau hyn. Hefyd, deuir ar draws rhai ffurflenni 38 na chwblhawyd yn ôl argymhellion Côd Gweithrediad y Ddeddf. Y mae'r Comisiwn yn pwysleisio'r pwysigrwydd o weithredu'r rhan hon o'r Ddeddf yn gywir.

Ploblemau Asesu'r Galw am Dderbyniad Gorfodol i Ysbyty

Y mae dod i benderfyniad ynglŷn â'r galw am dderbyniad gorfodol person i ysbyty yn un anodd a blin i'r person hwnnw a'i deulu. Heblaw am farn y meddyg teulu, yn y mwyafrif o achosion dibynnir ar farn dau berson arall, meddyg arall, sydd wedi ei gymeradwyo oherwydd ei 'brofiad arbennig mewn diagnosis a thriniaeth afiechyd meddwl' [adran 12(2) o Ddeddf Iechyd Meddwl 1983], a gweithiwr cymdeithasol, a gymeradwywyd o dan adran 114 o'r Ddeddf. Yn wir, os penderfynir gwneud cais am dderbyniad gorfodol, yn y mwyafrif o achosion ni ellir cwblhau'r ffurflenni cyfreithiol angenrheidiol hebddynt.

Fodd bynnag, yn rhai siroedd, y tu allan i amserau a dyddiau gwaith, y mae anawsterau wrth geisio darpar gwasanaeth gweithwyr cymdeithasol a gymeradwywyd. Yn aml y mae tîmau argyfwng yn gyfrifol am wasanaeth dros yr holl sir ar yr amserau hyn, ac anawsterau ar brydiau oherwydd pellter mawr rhai galwadau. Yn un o'r siroedd hefyd, am gyfnod o flwyddyn a rhagor, ni ddarparwyd gwasanaeth o gwbl dros oriau'r nos, a hyn, o bryd i bryd, yn achosi problemau enbyd i'r claf, ei deulu, meddygon teulu a'r heddlu. Cyfrifoldeb y llywodraethau lleol yw sicrhau gwasanaeth gwethwyr cymdeithasol bedair awr ar hugain, er mwyn cwrdd â gofynion y Ddeddf Iechyd Meddwl pryd bynnag y bo galw.

Y mae prinder meddygon a gymeradwywyd o dan adran 12(2) o'r Ddeddf yn broblem mewn nifer o ardalaoedd hefyd. Yn un sir ymddengys mae'r prinder hwn yw'r prif reswm dros y nifer mawr o dderbyniadau gorfodol o dan adran 4 o'r Ddeddf, sy'n caniatau derbyiadau gydag un argymhelliad meddygol, yn lle'r ddau arferol. Pwrpas adran 4 yw galluogi cwrdd â gofynion achosion brys, pan fyddai gorfod aros rhai oriau am yr ail feddyg yn beryglus. Camddefnydd enbyd o adran 4, er enghraifft, yw ei ddefnyddio oherwydd na ellir disgwyl meddyg adran 12(2) am 3 diwrnod, fel y dywedwyd mewn un achos.

Cyfrifoldeb yr Awdurdod Iechyd Dosbarth yw sicrau fod digon o feddygon adran 12(2) ar gael, a bod rhestr gyfoes ohonynt ar gael i wethwyr cymdeithasol. Y mae'r Comisiwn yn tanlinellu'r pwysigrwydd o asesiad gan feddyg â phrofiad ym maes afiechyd meddwl wrth drafod a ddylid wneud cais am dderbyniad gorfodol neu beidio.

Section VI

Appendices

1 The Statutory Responsibilities of the Commission

The Mental Health Act Commission is a Special Health Authority established in 1983. It comprises some 90 part time members, including lay persons, lawyers, doctors, nurses, social workers, psychologists, and other specialists (see Appendix 6 for list of members).

1.1 Review of Powers and Duties

The Commission's central statutory responsibility, on behalf of the Secretary of State, is to keep under review the use of the Mental Health Act 1983 (the Act), which it does primarily by interviewing patients detained, or liable to be detained, under the Act.

The Commission carries out its responsibilities by undertaking an annual programme of visits to hospitals and Registered Mental Nursing Homes which admit detained patients.

Further information on this topic can be found in Chapter 9.

1.2 The Code of Practice

Section 118 of the Mental Health Act requires the Secretary of State to produce a Mental Health Act Code of Practice and to consult with any concerned bodies before making amendments to the Code. At the beginning of 1990 the Secretary of State asked the Commission to monitor the implementation of the Code of Practice and to advise Ministers of any changes to the Code which the Commission feels might be appropriate.

1.3 The Investigation of Complaints

Section 120 of the Mental Health Act empowers the Commission to investigate complaints in the following circumstances:

- any complaint made by a person in respect of a matter that occurred while he was detained under this Act in a hospital or Registered Mental Nursing Home and which he considers has not been satisfactorily dealt with by the Managers of that hospital or Registered Mental Nursing Home or;

- any other complaint as to the exercise of the powers or the discharge of the duties conferred or imposed by this Act in respect of a person who is or has been so detained.

1.4 Withholding of Mail

Section 121 (7) of the Act empowers the Commission to review, if requested to do so by the patient or by the person sending a postal packet, any Managers' decisions made under Section 134 to withhold from a detained patient the packet or its contents.

1.5 Consent to Treatment

The Commission is required under Section 121(2)(a) to appoint;

- registered medical practitioners to give Second Opinions in cases where this is required by the Act

- other persons to certify capacity to consent under Section 57 of the Act.

The Commission also receives and examines reports on treatment given under the consent to treatment provisions (Section 61).

1.6 Publication of a Biennial Report

Section 121(10) specifies that the Commission must publish a biennial report on its activities which it sends to the Secretary of State, who ensures that a copy is laid before both Houses of Parliament.

1.7 General Policy Advice

The Commission offers advice to Ministers on matters falling within its remit. In particular the Commission meets annually with the Minister and has a specific opportunity, at this point, to raise priority policy issues. This does not, of course, preclude the Commission from raising matters of concern with the Minister in the interim.

STATUTORY INSTRUMENTS

1983 No. 892

NATIONAL HEALTH SERVICE, ENGLAND AND WALES

The Mental Health Act Commission (Establishment and Constitution) Order 1983

Made	17th June 1983
Laid before Parliament	1st July 1983
Coming into Operation	
Articles 1, 2 and 4	1st September 1983
Remainder	30th September 1983

The Secretary of State for Social Services, in exercise of the powers conferred upon him by section 11 of the National Health Service Act 1977(a), and of all other powers enabling him in that behalf, hereby makes the following order:

Citation, commencement and interpretation

1   (1) This order may be cited as the Mental Health Act Commission (Establishment and Constitution) Order 1983 and shall come into operation on 1st September 1983 except that Article 3 shall come into operation on 30th September 1983.

(2) In this order –

"the Act" means the Mental Health Act 1983(b);

"the Commission" means the Commission established by Article 2 of this Order.

Establishment of the Commission

2   There is hereby established a special health authority which shall be known as the Mental Health Act Commission

Functions of the Commission

3   (1) Subject to and in accordance with such directions as the Secretary of State may give to the Commission, the Commission shall, in addition to performing its functions specified in the Act, perform on behalf of the Secretary of State the functions specified in paragraph (2) of this Article and such other functions as the Secretary of State may direct.

(a) 1977 c. 49; section 11(1) was amended by the Health Services Act 1980 (c. 53), Schedule 1, paragraph 31.

(b) 1983 c. 20.

---

(2) the functions of the Secretary of State referred to in paragraph (1) above are –

(a) the function of appointing registered medical practitioners for the purposes of Part IV of the Act (consent to treatment) and section 118 of the Act (practitioners required to certify consent and to give second opinion) and of appointing other persons for the purposes of section 57(2)(a) of the Act (persons required to certify consent);

(b) the functions of the Secretary of State under section 61 of the Act (review of treatment);

(c) the functions of the Secretary of State under section 120(1) and (4) of the Act (general protection of patients detained under the Act); and

(d) the function of submitting to the Secretary of State proposals as to the content of the code of practice which he shall prepare, and from time to time revise, under section 118(1) of the Act, and in particular to propose, for the purposes of section 118(2) of the Act, forms of medical treatment in addition to any specified in regulations made for the purposes of section 57 of the Act which in the opinion of the Commission give rise to special concern.

Constititution of the Commission

4 The Commission shall consist of such number of members as the Secretary of State may from time to time determine of whom one shall be the chairman and one vice-chairman.

Norman Fowler,
Secretary of State for Social Services

17th June 1983.

EXPLANATORY NOTE

(This Note is not part of the Order)

This Order provides for the establishment, as required by section 56(1) of the Mental Health (Amendment) Act 1982 (c. 51), and the constitution of a special health authority, to be known as the Mental Health Act Commission, to exercise functions under the Mental Health Act 1983, including the appointment of medical practitioners and other persons for the purposes of that Act, the review of treatment, the general protection of patients detained under that Act and the submission to the Secretary of State of proposals for the preparation and revision of a Code of Practice.

1983 No. 894

NATIONAL HEALTH SERVICE, ENGLAND AND WALES

The Mental Health Act Commission Regulations 1983

Made	17th June 1983
Laid before Parliament	1st July 1983
Coming into Operation	1st September 1983

The Secretary of State for Social Services, in exercise of the powers conferred upon him by section 12 of Schedule 5 to the National Health Service Act 1977(a), and of all other powers enabling him in that behalf, hereby makes the following regulations:

Citation, commencement and interpretation

1 (1) These regulations may be cited as the Mental Health Act Commission Regulations 1983 and shall come into operation on 1st September 1983.

(2) In these regulations, unless the context otherwise requires –

"the Commission" means the Mental Health Act Commission establish by the Order;

"the Order" means the Mental Health Act Commission (Establishment and Constitution) Order 1983(b).

Appointment of chairman and members

2 The chairman and members of the Commission shall be appointed by the Secretary of State.

Tenure of office of chairman and members

3 Subject to the following provisions of these regulations and to any provisions of regulations applied by these regulations, the term of office of the chairman or a member shall be such period, not exceeding four years, as the Secretary of State may specify on making the appointment

Termination of tenure of office

4 (1) The chairman or a member of the Commission may resign his office at any time during the period for which he was appointed by giving notice in writing to the Secretary of State.

(a) 1977 c. 49.   (b) S.I. 1983/892.

(2) Notwithstanding that the appointment of the chairman or any member is for a term of years, the Secretary of State may, at any time, terminate that person's tenure of office.

Eligibility for re-appointment

5   Subject to any provisions of regulations applied by these regulations as to disqualification from membership, the chairman or a member of the Commission shall, on the termination of his tenure of office, be eligible for re-appointment.

Vice-chairman

6   (1) The Secretary of State may appoint a member of the Commission to be vice-chairman for such period as the Secretary of State may specify on making the appointment.

(2) Where no such appointment is made, the chairman and members of the Commission shall elect one of their number, other than the chairman, to be vice-chairman for a period of one year or, where the period of his membership during which he is elected has less than a year to run, for the remainder of such period.

(3) Any members so appointed or elected may at any time resign from the office of vice-chairman by giving notice in writing –

(a) if he was appointed by the Secretary of State, to the Secretary of State;

(b) in any other case, to the chairman of the Commission,

and the Secretary of State may thereupon appoint another member or, failing such an appointment, the chairman and members shall thereupon elect another member as vice-chairman in accordance with paragraph (1) or, as the case may be, paragraph (2) of this regulation.

Committees and sub-committees

7   (1) The Secretary of State shall appoint a central policy committee of the Commission, consisting wholly of members of the Commission, but the Commission may co-opt any other members of the Commission as a member of the committee.

(2) Subject to paragraph (3) of this regulation and subject to and in accordance with such directions as the Secretary of State may give to that committee, the central policy committee shall perform on behalf of the Commission the following functions: –

(a) the function mentioned in Article 3(2)(d) of the Order (proposals for the code of practice:;

(b) the preparation of the report on the Commission's activities required by section 121(10) of the Mental Health Act 1983(a);

(c) any other function, or activity in connection with any function, which the Commission may require it to perform.

(a) S.I. 1983 c. 20.

---

(3) The functions mentioned in paragraph (2)(a) and (b) of this regulation, and any such function under paragraph (2)(c) of this regulation as the Commission may specify, shall be performed in consultation with the Commission.

(4) Subject to such directions as may be given by the Secretary of State, the Commission may, and if so directed shall, appoint committees of the Commission, consisting wholly of members of the Commission.

(5) A committee appointed under this regulation may, subject to such directions as may be given by the Secretary of State or the Commission appoint sub-committees consisting wholly of members of the Commission.

(6) Any power in this regulation to appoint members of the Commission as members of any committee or sub-committee shall include the power to appoint the chairman as a member of such a committee or sub-committee.

Meetings and proceedings

8   (1) The meetings and proceedings of the Commission shall be conducted in accordance with Standing Orders made under paragraph (2) of this regulation.

(2) Subject to paragraph (3) of this regulation, the Commission shall make, and may vary or revoke, Standing Orders for the regulation of their proceedings and business and provision may be made in those Standing Orders for the suspension of those Orders.

(3) The Standing Orders shall provide that there shall be held at least one full meeting of the Commission in any year.

Application or regulations relating to membership

9   The provisions of regulation 7 (disqualification for appointment) and regulation 8 (cessation of disqualification) of the National Health Service (Regional and District Health Authorities: Membership and Procedure) Regulations 1983(a) shall apply as if any reference in those regulations to an Authority included a reference to the Commission.

Norman Fowler,
Secretary of State for Social Services

(a) 1983/315.

2 Other Activities of the Commission

2.1 Financial Control

The Mental Health Act Commission, as a Special Health Authority, is financed directly by the Department of Health, with a contribution from the Welsh Office. A summary of the Commission's finances is given at Appendix 3.

The Commission achieved "independent budget status" from 1 April 1995. This means that although the Commission continues to get direct funding from the Department of Health, it now has more freedom in deciding how the money should be spent.

The Commission's expenditure is closely monitored by a subgroup of the Central Policy Committee, and its accounts are audited by the Audit Commission. The Commission currently accounts for its expenditure on the date invoices are received. This will change from 1996 when the Commission moves to accrual based accounting.

The Commission will also introduce Standing Financial Instructions and an Internal Audit Committee with effect from 1 November 1995. This will ensure that all financial aspects of its operation will meet with the requirements of the Code of Conduct and Accountability for NHS Boards.

2.2 Conferences

The Commission has held regular Conferences for Commission members over the last two years, as required by Regulation 8, usually in October and April. These Conferences traditionally combine the business activities of the Commission with a training session for Commission members on a chosen topic.

2.3 Training

Commission members are frequently invited to participate in training events, which they do willingly.

In addition, the Chief Executive has continued to undertake training sessions, particularly in relation to the Mental Health Act Code of Practice.

Because of the recent large increase in number of Commission members appointed, as part of its restructuring exercise (Chapter 1), the Commission has mounted its own extensive training programme for new members. In all, approximately 134 new members have received four days of training.

2.4   The Commission And Research

The Commission's Fifth Biennial Report explained that, in carrying out its statutory duties it acquires a considerable amount of information that could be used as a subject for high quality academic research. The Commission has no budget or resources for undertaking research of its own but has continued to support research proposals from other organisations and to make its facilities available to researchers.

The Commission has entered into negotiations with Nottingham University about collaboration between the Commission and the University on research. The Commission has suggested that a joint audit, making full use of the research and policy expertise residing in the University, could usefully be undertaken to identify;

- data currently being received or generated by the Commission
- any desirable additional data
- how the Commission could adjust its procedures to improve the collection and handling of data to;
- enhance the undertaking of its statutory responsibilities
- make such data more accessible to independent researchers

The outcome of this initiative is still awaited at the time of drafting this report.

2.5   Liaison with other Agencies

- **The Commission liaises with; The National Trust Federation, and National Association of Health Authorities and Trusts**

   The Commission held meetings with both the National Trust Federation and the National Association of Health Authorities and Trusts to discuss matters of mutual interest. It is anticipated that links with these two organisations will be retained in the future.

- **Mental Health Review Tribunals**

  In its previous Biennial Report the Commission reported on its shared concern with the Council on Tribunals about the delay in processing Mental Health Review Tribunals. The Commission, as a matter of policy, does not become directly involved in matters concerning Tribunals but it continues to maintain a general interest in their work and useful links with the Tribunal offices. The Commission is aware that there have been a range of Department of Health initiatives which have succeeded in reducing the delays in processing Section 3 Tribunals.

- **Health Commissioning Authorities**

  Commission members and Health Commissioners have formed a group to discuss matters of policy and practice which have arisen out of the reorganisation of the NHS. The group will probably meet on an annual basis. Arising from this group's deliberations, the Commission has developed a pack for commissioning authorities to aid in the development of quality standards.

- **Association of Directors of Social Services**

  The Chief Executive and a Commission member participated in a workshop at the Annual Social Services Conference in April 1994.

- **Special Hospitals Services Authority (SHSA)**

  The Commission has continued to meet with the SHSA twice a year. This provides a useful forum for discussing issues of concern. The Commission and SHSA have embarked on a joint project to develop quality standards.

- **Home Office**

  The Commission has regular contacts with the Home Office, usually in relation to individual patient issues with whom both organisations have an interest. Within the previous two years however, the Home Office hosted an informative visit for Commission staff.

  The Commission was also in correspondence with the Home Office about the introduction by the Home Secretary of the requirement for RMO's to notify him before restricted patients are allowed Section 17 leave to holiday facilities (See Chapter 9.4)

- **Association of Metropolitan Authorities**

  The Chief Executive and a Commission Member met with the Association of Metropolitan Authorities to discuss the latter's inquiry into the role of ASW's after the implementation of the purchaser/provider split in local authorities.

- **Royal College of Psychiatrists**

  The Commission has commented on the draft document produced by the College in relation to the criteria for approval and training of Section 12 doctors. The Commission supported the proposals for revising the criteria for appointment, for the introduction of mandatory and refresher training.

The Chairman and Vice Chairman have also discussed with the College the heavy workload of forensic psychiatrists in the Special Hospitals.

It is clear to the Commission that the College is committed to enhancing psychiatrists' knowledge of the Mental Health Act and the Commission has indicated that it is prepared to help in this process, as far as its resources allow.

2.6 Provision Of Advice

The Commission continues to receive numerous requests for advice on a large range of issues and a large number of groups, particularly from mental health professionals and administrators. The Commission has no remit to give legal advice, but always tries to be of assistance by talking through possible alternative courses of action.

The Commission has continued to add to its list of practice notes, which now includes one on Registered Mental Nursing Homes, and use of Section 17 leave. A practice note on irregularities in applications for detention under the Act and a briefing note for GPs are also in the final stages of preparation.

3 Summary of Finances, including Audited Accounts for 1994-1995

Mental Health Act Commission Expenditure 1993-94

- Commission Fees and Expenses
- Second Opinion Appointed Doctors Fees and Expenses
- Staff Salaries
- Non-manpower Expenditure
- Second Opinion Appointed Doctor Training

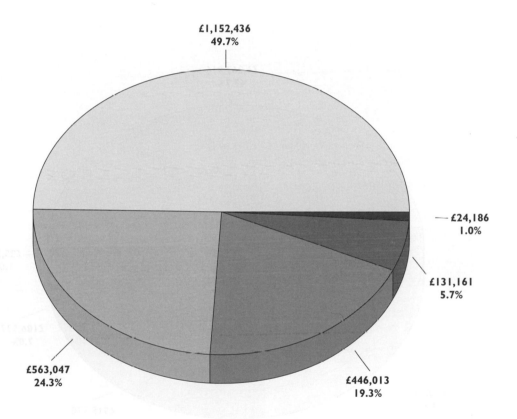

£1,152,436
49.7%

£24,186
1.0%

£131,161
5.7%

£563,047
24.3%

£446,013
19.3%

1st April 1993 – 31st March 1994: Total Expenditure = £2,316,843

Mental Health Act Commission Expenditure 1994-95

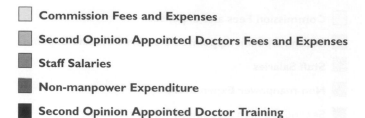

- Commission Fees and Expenses
- Second Opinion Appointed Doctors Fees and Expenses
- Staff Salaries
- Non-manpower Expenditure
- Second Opinion Appointed Doctor Training

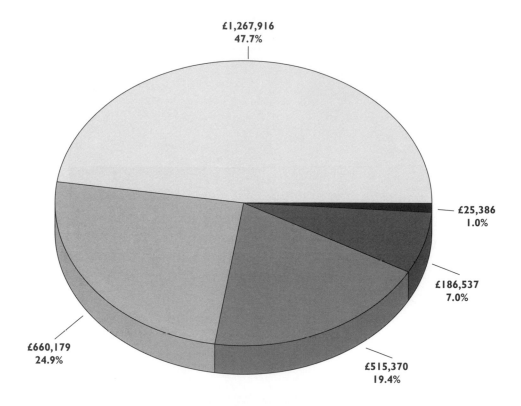

£1,267,916
47.7%

£25,386
1.0%

£186,537
7.0%

£515,370
19.4%

£660,179
24.9%

1st April 1994 – 31st March 1995: Total Expenditure = £2,655,388

Statement of Chief Executive's Responsibilities in Respect of the Accounts

The Chief Executive is required under the National Health Services Act 1977 to prepare accounts for each financial year. The Secretary of State, with the approval of the Treasury, directs that these accounts present fairly the receipts and payments of the authority for that period. In preparing those accounts, the Chief Executive is required to:

- Apply on a consistent basis accounting policies laid down by the Secretary of State with the approval of the Treasury.

- Make judgements and estimates which are reasonable and prudent.

- State whether applicable accounting standards have been followed, subject to any material departures disclosed and explained in the account.

The Chief Executive confirms that they have complied with the above requirements in preparing the accounts.

The Chief Executive is responsible for keeping proper accounting records which disclose with reasonable accuracy at any time the financial position of the authority and to enable them to ensure that the accounts comply with requirements outlined in the above mentioned direction by the Secretary of State. They are also responsible for safeguarding the assets of the authority and hence for taking reasonable steps for the prevention and detection of fraud and other irregularities.

By Order of the Board

Signed: Chairman   Dated 27-9-19 95

Chief Executive   William Brophy   Date 27.9 1995

Statement of Finance Manager's Responsibilities

- The maintenance of financial records appropriate to the activities of the authority.

- The establishment and monitoring of a system of internal control.

- The establishment of arrangements for the prevention of fraud and corruption.

- The preparation of annual financial statements which present fairly the financial position of the authority and the results of its operations.

In fulfilment of these responsiblities I confirm the financial statements set out on pages 3 to 7 attached, have been compiled from and are in accordance with the financial records maintained by the authority and with the accounting standards and policies for the NHS approved by the Secretary of State.

Signed: Finance Manager   Dated *28/9/1995*

Auditor's Reports on the Health Authority Accounts

We certify that we have completed the audit of the financial statement on pages 3 to 7 attached, which have been prepared in accordance with the accounting policies relevant to the National Health Service.

Respective responsibilities of directors and auditors

As described above, the Chief Executive is responsible for the preparation of financial statements. It is our responsibility to form an independent opinion, based on our audit on those statements, and to report our opinion to you.

Basis of opinion

We carried out our audit in accordance with part 1 of the National Health Service and Community Care Act 1990 and the Code of Practice issued by the Audit Commission, which requires compliance with relevant auditing standards.

Our audit included examination, on a test basis, of evidence relevant to the amounts and disclosures in the financial statements. It also included an assessment of the significant estimates and judgements made by the authority in preparation of the financial statements, and of whether the accounting policies are appropriate to the authority's circumstances, consistently applied and adequately disclosed.

We planned and performed our audit so as to obtain all the information and explanations which we considered necessary in order to provide us with sufficient evidence to give reasonable assurance that the financial statements are free from material misstatement, whether caused by fraud or other irregularity or error. In forming our opinion we also evaluated the overall adequacy of the presentation of information in the financial statements.

Opinion

In our opinion the financial statements present fairly the receipts and payments of the Mental Health Act Commission for the year ended 31 March 1995.

Signed: Auditor   [signature]   Dated 28/9 19 95

Mental Health Act Commission Special Health Authority

Receipts and Payments Accounts for the Period
1 April 1994 - 31 March 1995

Receipts

	Notes	1994-1995	1993-1994
Cash Advances from DH	3	£2,650,886.00	£2,370,149.00
Other receipts		£13,297.00	£4,742.00
Patient Information Leaflet Sponsorhsip		£3,141.00	
		£2,667,324.00	£2,374,891.00

Payments

	Notes	1994-1995	1993-1994
Salaries	4	£515,368.00	£446,013.00
Other Operating Payments	5	£2,136,878.00	£1,923,280.00
Patient Information Leaflet Sponsorhsip		£3,141.00	
		£2,665,387.00	£2,369,293.00

	1994-1995	1993-1994
Surplus (Deficit) from operations	£11,937.00	£5,598.00
Other Receipts/Payments	–	–
Appropriations	–	–

EXCESS OF RECEIPTS OVER PAYMENTS
(PAYMENTS OVER RECEIPTS)

	1994-1995	1993-1994
	£11,937.00	£5,598.00

Mental Health Act Commission Special Health Authority

Statement of Balances as at 31 March 1995

	Notes	1994-1995	1993-1994
Balance at beginning of year		£14,418.00	£8,820.00
Return of 1993/94 receipts		-£4,742.00	–
Excess Receipts over payment		£11,937.00	£5,598.00
Amount returned to Department		-£11,937.00	
Difference between cash held at 31 March 1994 and 1995		-£1,360.00	
Balance at 31 March 1995	6	£8,316.00	£14,418.00

The notes on Pages 175, 176 & 177 form part of these accounts.

Mental Health Act Commission Special Health Authority

Notes to the accounts

a) These accounts are drawn up in a form directed by the Secretary of State and approved by the Treasury.

b) The figure of advances from Class XIII Vote 3 C3(3a) includes a tax payment of £176,000.00, the precise breakdown of which is awaited from Department of Health. The liability to the tax is in respect of financial years 1994/1995 and arises from the payment of expenses to Commissioners by the Department of Health (See Note 7).

For 1994/1995 actual figures were extracted from the accounting records of the Department of Health for all items disclosed in Notes 3, 4 and 5:-

- All balance of funds at the end of each financial year are retained by the Department of Health. Therefore the 1994/95 accounts show return of receipts relating to the 1993/94 financial year. Receipts are now shown as being received and returned in the same financial year.

Receipts

	1994-1995	1993-1994
a - Advances from Class XIII Vote 3 C3	£1,953,481.00	£1,739,669.00
b - Advances from Class XIII Vote 3 A1 9	£698,705.00	£577,272.00
c - Advances from Welsh Office	–	£52,450.00
d - Advances from (Refunds to) Class XIII Vote 3 Suspense Account	£1,300.00	£758.00
Other receipts	£13,297.00	£4,742.00
Patient information Leaflet Sponsorship	£3,141.00	–
	£2,667,324.00	£2,374,891.00

Salaries

	1994-1995	1993-1994
a - Staff Salaries	£426,799.00	£359,815.00
b - National Insurance Contribution		
– Employer	£30,751.00	£27,190.00
c - Superannuation	£53,766.00	£48,011.00
d - Agency Costs	£4,052.00	£10,997.00
	£515,368.00	£446,013.00

Other operating payments

	1994-1995	1993-1994
a - Accommodation	£64,793.00	£62,446.00
b - Stationery, telephone, postage, common services, travel & subsistence etc.	£107,125.00	£58,734.00
c - Payments for purchase, construction or adaptation of premises	£1,888.00	£1,841.00
d - Plant and equipment	£9,591.00	£8,140.00
e - Members' Fees and Expenses	£1,179,894.00	£1,138,126.00
f - Second Opinion Doctors' Fees and Expenses	£660,179.00	£563,047.00
g - Miscellaneous Expenditure	£88,022.00	£66,760.00
h - SOAD Training	£25,386.00	£24,186.00
i - Patient Information Leaflet	£3,141.00	
	£2,140,019.00	£1,923,280.00

Cash balance at 31 March

	1994-1995	1993-1994
a - Cash held by Members	£8,183.00	£9,483.00
b - Cash at Bank	NIL	NIL
c - Cash in hand (Petty cash)	£133.00	£193.00
d - Other receipts		£4,742.00
	£8,316.00	£14,418.00

Cash limits

The accounts of Health Authorities are subject to cash limit controls. A Cash limit is a predetermined limit on the spending (in cash terms) of Health Authorities. Each Health Authority is required to contain its net revenue outgoings or net capital payments in the year within the approved cash limit. In the particular case of the Mental Health Act Commission Special Health Authority, all expenditure has been subject to notified cash limits with the exception of the accommodation charges, which remains funded centrally by the Department of Health, and the Patient Information Leaflet Sponsorship Fund which does not form part of the cash limit.

A statement of net over/underspending of this Authority against the approved cash limit for the year ended 31 March is set out below:

	Revenue 1994-1995	Revenue 1993-1994
Cash Limit	£2,617,000.00	£1,761,450.00
Charge against Cash Limit	£2,587,453.00	£1,792,119.00
Underspending	£29,547.00	–
Overspending	–	£30,669.00

The Mental Health Act Commission

Accounts Direction

The Secretary of State, with the approval of the Treasury, in pursuance of Section 98(2) of the National Health Service Act 1977 hereby gives the following direction:

> In this direction, unless the context otherwise requires:-
>
> "the Act" means the National Health Service Act 1977;
>
> "the Commission" means the Mental Health Act Commission.

Form of accounts

The statement of accounts which it is the duty of the Commission to prepare in respect of the financial year ended 31 March 1995 shall be as set out in the following paragraphs and Schedule.

Accounts of the commission

The statement of accounts of the Commission shall comprise:

 a a foreword;

 b a receipts and payments accounts;

 c a statement of cash and bank balances;

 d such notes as may be necessary for the purposes referred to in paragraph 4 below.

The statement of accounts shall properly present the receipts and payments for the year and the cash and bank balances as at the end of the financial year. Subject to the foregoing requirements, the statement of accounts shall also, without limiting the information given and as described in the Schedule, meet:

 a all relevant guidance given in *"Government Accounting"* and in *"Trading Accounts : A Guide for Government Departments and Non-Departmental Public Bodies"* and in the *"NHS Manual for Accounts"*, modified as appropriate;

 b any disclosure and accounting requirements which the Secretary of Stater or Treasury may issue from time to time;

insofar as these are appropriate to the Commission and are in force for the financial period for which the statement of accounts is to be prepared.

This accounts direction supersedes that dated 10 September 1993.

Dated   11ᵗ April 1995

Signed by the authority of the Secretary of State for Health

Signed

J M Brownlee
Assistant Secretary
Department of Health

Schedule

Foreword

1 The foreword shall include a statement that the account has been prepared in accordance with a direction given by the Secretary of State.

2 The foreword shall describe the statutory background and main functions of the Commission.

3 The foreword shall be dated and signed by the Chairman and the Chief Executive of the Commission.

Receipts and Payments Account and Statement of Cash & Bank Balances

4 The receipts shall be analysed by Class(es) and Number(s) of the Vote(s) showing also the sub-headings of the Vote(s). Resources made available from sources other than the Department of Health shall be identified separately.

5 Payments shall be analysed into appropriate headings, distinguishing payments for the purchase, construction or adaptation of premises and for plant and equipment from other types of payments.

6 The Chairman and the Chief Executive of the Commission shall sign and date the financial statements immediately after the statement of cash and bank balances.

Notes to the Accounts

7 The notes to the accounts shall, inter alia, include details of the accounting policies adopted.

8 Notes providing further explanations of figures in the accounts shall be made where it is considered appropriate for a proper understanding of the accounts.

9 The accounts direction shall be reproduced as an appendix to the accounts.

4.1 Psychosurgery

Operating Centres

The main focus of psychosurgery in this country continues to be the Brook Hospital, but a small number of operations are carried out at the University Hospital of Wales in Cardiff, Atkinson Morley's Hospital in London and Pinderfields Hospital in Wakefield. The operative procedures used are as follows.

Brook	- Stereotactic subcaudate tractotomy
Atkinson Morley's	- Limbic leucotomy
Univ. Hosp. of Wales	- Bilateral capsulotomy
Pinderfields	- Stereotactic bifrontal leucotomy

Number of Operations Referred and Performed

The total number of patients referred to the Commission, i.e. visits undertaken, in the period under review (1/7/93 to 30/6/95) was 30. This number is significantly lower than in previous years (1991-93 46, 1989-91 52,1985-87 54, 1983-85 57). The number of subsequent operations carried out was 24. On six occasions the Commission's appointed team did not sign the form 37 - four of these resulted from the patient withdrawing their consent at the time of the visit. Two of these six cases necessitated later revisits, one of which resulted in certification.

The main centres specialising in the work covered by Section 57 are given in Table 1:

Table 1

Brook Hospital	15 operations
Atkinson Morley's Hospital	5 operations
University Hospital of Wales	4 operations
Pinderfields Hospital	0 operations
Number of operations	24

Analysis of Referrals by Gender

Table 2 shows that more females than males were referred under Section 57.

Table 2

Male	8
Female	22
Total	30

Analysis of Section 61 Reports

Documentation, mainly consisting of team reports, discharge summaries and Section 61 reports in relation to 34 cases, were recently considered by the Commission. The prerequisite for a case to be monitored was the existence of a Section 61 report. The statistical information obtained is presented below:

Operating Centres

Brook	27
Atkinson Morley's	4
Pinderfields	2
University Hospital of Wales	1
Total	34

Age

20-30 years of age	1
31-40	12
41-50	10
51-60	8
61-70	2
71+	1
Total	34

Gender

Female	21
Male	13
Total	34

Illness

Bipolar Affective Disorder	2
Depression	18
Obsessional Disorder	12
Anxiety State	2
Total	34

Overseas Referrals (4 of 34)

USA	2
Republic of Ireland	1
Northern Ireland	1

4.2 Analyses of Section 58 Second Opinion Requests

Table 1   Section 58 – Second Opinion Requests July 1st 1993 – June 30th 1995

Section	Number	%
2	545	5
3	8,535	79
37	819	7.6
Other	903	8.4
Total	10,802	100

Table 2

Treatment	Number	%
Medicines	6,195	57.4
ECT	4,453	41.2
Both	154	1.4
Total	10,802	100

Table 3

Gender	Number	%
Male	5,332	49
Female	5,470	51
Total	10,802	100

Table 4

Gender	Medication		ECT		Both	
	Number	%	Number	%	Number	%
Male	3,936	64	1,344	30	56	36
Female	2,259	36	3,109	70	98	64
Total	6,195	100	4,453	100	154	100

Table 5

MHA Category	Number	%
Mental Illness	10,046	93
Mental Impairment	399	3.7
Severe Mental Impairment	185	1.7
Psychopathic Disorder	172	1.6
Totals	10,802	100

Table 6

R.H.A.	Mental Illness	Mental Impairment	Severe Mental Impairment	Psychopathic Disorder	Total Number
East Anglia	89.3	8.1	2.2	0.4	504
N.E. Thames	95.7	2	0.4	1.9	957
Oxford	89.3	5.4	2.1	3.2	559
N.W. Thames	93.2	3.3	2.2	1.3	769
S.E. Thames	95.3	2.8	0.7	1.1	811
S.W. Thames	94.5	2.7	1.5	1.3	523
Wessex	95.3	1.3	2.7	0.7	147
South Western	95.9	1.5	1.2	1.4	868
Northern	86.9	9.6	2.6	0.9	460
Yorkshire	92.4	5	1.2	1.4	808
Trent	95.5	1.3	2.5	0.7	710
West Midlands	96.6	1.7	1.3	0.4	979
Wales	97.2	1.5	0.8	0.5	398
North Western	96.3	2.2	0.7	0.8	1,199
Mersey	97.5	1.5	0	1	195
Speical Hospitals Service Authority					
Ashworth	77.9	2.7	2.3	17.1	257
Broadmoor	95	0.8	0	4.2	237
Rampton	70.8	18.3	10.2	0.7	421
Total	10,046 (92%)	399 (4%)	185 (2%)	172 (2%)	10,802 (100%)

The Mental Health Act Commission: Sixth Biennial Report 1993–1995

5 *List of Section 58 Appointed Doctors*

July 1993 - June 1995

Dr M Abou Saleh	Dr H Edwards	Dr T Kerr	Dr E Richards
Dr P Abraham	Dr S Edwards	Dr K Khan	Dr J Roberts
Dr M Alldrick	Dr A Fairburn	Dr D Kohen	Dr J Robertson
Dr J Annear	Dr G Feggetter	Dr L Kremer	Dr A Rugg
Dr D Battin	Dr T Fenton	Dr J Langley	Dr P Saleem
Dr S Baxter	Dr S Fernando	Dr M Launer	Dr M Salih
Dr S Benbow	Dr J Fisher	Dr L Liebling	Dr P Salmons
Dr K Bergman	Dr M Forth	Dr B Lowe	Dr G Sampson
Dr M Bethell	Dr A Francis	Dr J Lyon	Dr P Sarkar
Dr K Bhakta	Dr R Gall	Dr S Malik	Dr N Sebaratnum
Dr E Birchall	Dr D Gasper	Dr P Mars	Dr M Segal
Dr A Black	Dr A Ghosh	Dr G MAthur	Dr Silverman
Prof R Bluglass	Dr C Ghosh	Dr M Matthews	Dr J Slater
Dr J Bolton	Dr N Gittleson	Dr J McHugh	Dr Z Slattery
Dr N Bouras	Dr E Gordon	Dr L Measey	Dr S Soni
Dr C Boyd	Dr E Gregg	Dr G Mehta	Dr D Stephens
Dr A Bradfield	Dr J Grimshaw	Dr I Mian	Dr R Symonds
Dr O Briscoe	Dr J Hailstone	Dr G Milner	Dr L Tarlo
Dr C Brook	Dr M Harper	Dr N MIlton	Dr R Thavasothy
Dr A Burke	Dr J Harrington	Dr Minto	Dr R Thaya-Paran
Dr C Calvert	Dr B Harwin	Dr J Mumford	Dr I Thompson
Dr M Cashman	Dr A Hauck	Dr H Myers	Dr R Toms
Dr P Choudhary	Dr B Heine	Dr G Nanayakkara	Dr N Tyre
Dr A Clarkson	Dr P Hettiaratchy	Dr D Neal	Dr H Verma
Dr J Cockburn	Dr O Hill	Dr T Nelson	Dr G Wallen
Dr R Cope	Dr L Homwood	Dr H Nissenbaum	Dr A Walsh
Dr S Craske	Dr E Howarth	Dr J Noble	Dr D Ward
Dr D Cronin	Dr J Hughes	Dr M O'Brian	Dr P Watson
Dr J Cuthill	Dr R Hughes	Dr S Olivieri	Dr M Way
Dr C Davies	Dr J Hurst	Dr R F Orr	Dr K Weeks
Dr M Davies	Dr J Hutchinson	Dr F Oyebode	Dr J Whitehead
Dr N Davies	Dr G Ibrahimi	Dr M A Palejwala	Dr G Wijeyeratne
Dr J Davis	Dr H James	Dr S S Palia	Dr Y Wiley
Dr K Davison	Dr S James	Dr J Phillips	Dr D Williams
Dr K Day	Dr P Jefferys	Dr R Philpott	Dr A Wilson
Dr J Denmark	Dr J Jenkins	Dr I Pryce	Dr S Wood
Dr N Desai	Dr B John	Dr P Rack	Dr E Wright

Appendix: List of Section 58 Appointed Doctors

Dr R Devine

Dr D Dick

Dr G Duborg

Dr D Dunleavy

Dr H Eaton

Dr D Jones

Dr A Kaeser

Dr G Kanakaratnam

Dr A Kellam

Dr H Kelly

Dr C Rastogi

Dr B Rathod

Dr A Regan

Dr N Renton

Dr M Rice

Dr A Zigmond

6 *Mental Health Act Commission Members 1993-95*

CHAIRMAN:	Until 30/11/94 -	Sir Louis Blom-Cooper QC
	From 01/12/94 -	Viscountess R Runciman
VICE CHAIRMAN:	Until 31/12/94 -	Professor E Murphy
	From 01/01/95 -	Nigel Pleming QC

LAY

Dr M Barnes	Mr G Lakes	Ms J Rogers
Dr A Blowers	Mrs V Lipscombe	Mrs S Spence
Mrs M E Coleman	Mrs E Owen	Mrs B Stroll
Mrs P Entwistle	Mrs M Roberts	Mr M Taylor

LEGAL

Mrs C Bennett	Prof B Dimond	Mrs J Olsen
Mrs C Bond	Mr A Eldergill	Mr A Parkin
Mrs S Breach	Prof M Gunn	Ms L Sinclair
Miss P Cushing	Mrs M G Lloyd	

MEDICAL

Dr D Black	Dr P Hettiaratchy	Dr E Parker
Dr K Day	Dr J Holliday	Dr R Philpott
Dr D Dunleavy	Dr T Jerram	Dr I Pryce
Dr S Fernando	Dr G Mathur	Dr P Sebaratnam
Dr N Gittleson	Dr E Mendleson	Dr A Zigmond
Dr M Harper	Dr I Mian	

NURSING

Mr R Bevan	Mrs M Halliday	Mr A Morley
Mr P Brotherhood	Mrs S Lee	Mrs C Selim
Mr E Chitty	Mr N Lees	Mr A Persaud
Mr A Cooper	Miss G Linton	Mr B Thorne
Mr M Graham	Mr H McClarron	Mr R Wix

PSYCHOLOGY

Dr B Ashcroft	Ms P Spinks	Mr L Wilson
Mr A Dabbs	Mr D Torpy	Prof A Yates (deceased)
Mr J Sharich		

SOCIAL WORKER

Mr A Ball
Mr R Brown
Mr T Evans
Ms M Halstead

Mr G Halliday
Mr R Lingham
Mrs C Llewelyn-Jones

Miss I Nutting
Mr E Prtak
Mr A Williamson

SPECIALIST

Canon A Hawes
Mr G Lakes
Mrs L Mason
Mr A Milligan

Mr R North
Ms J Prior
Ms E Rassaby

Dr R Ryall
Mr N Weaver
Prof D West

7 | *Staffing Structure*

MHAC Staffing: as of 30/06/95

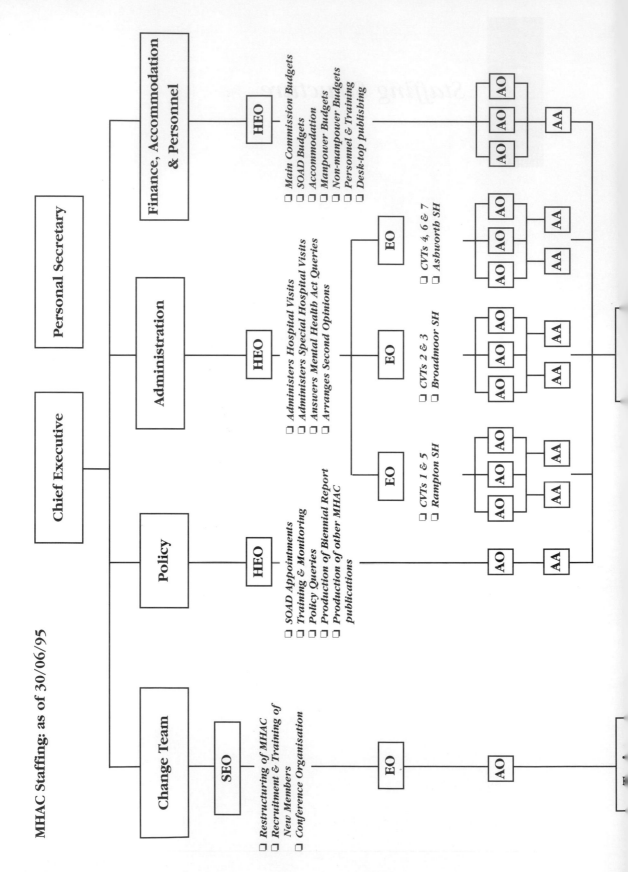

8 Commission Policies and Procedures

8.1 Visiting Policy

PART A
The Policy for Visiting Hospitals (Other Than Special Hospitals) and Mental Nursing Homes and for Meeting Representatives of Social Services Departments

1 The Commission Remit

The Commission's visiting remit is defined in the Mental Health Act 1983 as follows:-

"Section 120(1) - The Secretary of State will keep under review the exercise of the powers and the discharge of the duties conferred or imposed by this Act so far as relating to the detention of patients or to patients liable to be detained under this Act and shall make arrangements for persons authorised by him in that behalf -

  a. To visit and interview in private patients detained under this Act in hospitals and mental nursing homes;"

The Mental Health Act 1983 does not specifically authorise the Commission to visit Social Services Departments but meetings with departmental representatives are held in furtherance of the Commission's remit to keep under review the operation of the Act as it affects patients who are liable to be detained.

2 Access to Records

a NHS Hospitals

DHSS Circular HC(83)19 directs authorities to make arrangements to ensure that:-
  "Any records which are required to be made under the Mental Health (Hospitals, Guardianship and Consent to Treatment) Regulations 1983 (SI 1983/893) and which relate to the detention or treatment of a

patient of the hospital for which the authorities are responsible, are kept for a period of not less than five years commencing on the date on which the person to whom they relate ceases to be a patient in that hospital"

The Circular also empowers any person "authorised by the Mental Health Act Commission for the purposes of carrying out any review mentioned in Section 120(1) of the Mental Health Act 1983" to:-

"Require the production of and inspect any records relating to the detention or treatment of any person who is or has been detained in a hospital for which the authority is responsible".

b Registered Mental Nursing Homes

Any person appointed by the Mental Health Act Commission to carry out the functions set out in Section 120(1) may at any reasonable time "require the production of and inspect any records relating to the detention or treatment of any person who is or has been detained in a mental nursing home". (Section 120(4)(b)).

3 Purpose of Visits

a Hospitals and Registered Mental Nursing Homes

Visits by members of the Commission to hospitals and Registered Mental Nursing Homes have, broadly speaking, a fourfold purpose:-

  i. to meet with detained patients in private, particularly those who have asked to meet members of the Commission; meetings may be with individual patients or with groups of patients, including Patients Councils;
  ii. to observe the conditions in which patients are detained;
  iii. to see how the provisions of the Mental Health Act 1983 and the Code of Practice are being applied; and
  iv. to offer advice and guidance on the implementation of the Act.

b Social Services Departments

The purpose of meeting representatives of Social Services Departments is to encourage a co-ordinated approach to the operation of the Act and, in particular, to keep under review:-

  i. the Social Services Departments' responses to the Act and the Code of Practice,
  ii. the process of assessment, compulsory admission and detention under the Act, including the availability of ASWs; communication with GPs, hospitals, Section 12 doctors and the emergency services,

iii. the planning and delivery of appropriate residential places, alternatives to detention and aftercare procedures and facilities.

iv. the extent to which hospital and community services are able to integrate all aspects of a patient's detention from the initial assessment to the termination of aftercare.

To facilitate this process a number of Commission members and visiting members will be allocated to one or other of the Commission Visiting Teams (CVTs), each of which has a designated visiting area and is under the leadership of a Convenor who is appointed jointly by the Chairman and the Chief Executive of the Commission. All CVT members are expected to behave in such a way as to ensure that:

a. the dignity of all patients is respected;

b. the patients' legitimate concerns are considered equitably and pursued with vigour;

c. issues of race, culture, gender and disability are fully acknowledged and respected;

d. all patients are kept fully informed of any action taken by the Commission on their behalf;

e. records of interviews, meetings and issues raised by patients / clients are accurately maintained and that appropriate follow-up action is taken without delay; and

f. there is effective interaction with patients, the groups representing patients (including the Patients Council and the Advocacy Service, where they exist), the clinical staff and the Hospital Management Teams.

4 Frequency and Scope of Routine Visits

There are two main types of visit routinely undertaken by the Commission. One is the full visit which entails the prior receipt of a full range of background information, meetings with senior managers and other members of the staff, meetings with detained patients, visits to all areas and facilities available to them, and a formal feedback meeting at the end of the visit followed by a written report. Each hospital/mental nursing home will receive a full visit once every two years and, in some circumstances, more frequently.

The other type of visit is the patients-only visit, during which the main focus is on meetings with detained patients and more limited visits to the areas and facilities available to them. At the end of a patients-only visit there will normally be a formal feedback to the nominated liaison person only, rather than to a group meeting of senior managers. A brief summary report will be sent to the Chief

Executive shortly afterwards. Each hospital/Registered Mental Nursing Home will receive at least three patients-only visits in a two year period.

Regional/Medium Secure Units will be paid both a full visit and a patients-only visit at least once a year. Visits to Special Hospitals are regulated by a separate policy and procedure.

The duration of visits will be determined by the CVT Convenor who will take account of such factors as the number of detained patients, the size, nature and geographical distribution of the units to be visited and the experience of previous visits.

5   Targeted Visits

From time to time the Commission will undertake additional visits as part of targeted exercises or thematic reviews to examine particular issues such as the use of seclusion, bed occupancy, aftercare arrangements etc. These visits may be routinely notified, unannounced, short notice or out of hours visits.

6   Unannounced Visits

It is neither necessary nor desirable that prior notice should always be given of the Commission's intention to visit and at least 10% of the visits undertaken by each CVT must be unannounced. The CVT Executive Officer should always be told in advance when an unannounced visit is to take place.

Because of the lack of notice it is likely that access to personnel and to information will be either limited or delayed and the visiting arrangements should be modified accordingly.

7   Short Notice Visits

Circumstances may arise in which it is considered that, although an unannounced visit would not be appropriate, the unit to be visited should be given only very short notice of the Commission's intention to visit. In such cases, where the notice might be measured in hours rather than days, the limitations associated with unannounced visits may apply with almost equal force.

8   Out of Hours Visits

Arrangements may be made for members of the Commission to visit patients and/or facilities in the evenings or at weekends. Such visits will normally be patients-only visits and may be either routinely notified, unannounced or short notice visits.

9 Extended Visits

An extended visit may be necessary if essential work cannot be completed in the allotted time, for example, if there has been insufficient time to contact all the detained patients who have asked to meet a member of the Commission. In these exceptional circumstances, arrangements may be made for one or more members of the team to return the next day, or soon afterwards, to complete the work.

10 Additional Visits

There may be circumstances in which it is desirable for a hospital or Registered Mental Nursing Home to be visited in advance of, and in addition to, the next scheduled visit. An additional visit may be either notified or unannounced.

11 Composition of Visiting Teams

The aim is to provide a balanced visiting team in respect of both personal and professional skills and experience, taking into account the type of unit to be visited and the issues likely to arise. Other factors which must be taken into account when selecting a visiting team will include the gender and ethnic mix and the distances to be travelled. An experienced Commission member will be appointed to lead the visiting team, which will normally include not more than one newly appointed member of the Commission. At least one Commission member of the visiting team should have participated in the previous visit, either as the team leader or as a member of the team.

a Full Visits

A full visit will be carried out by a mixed team of members and visiting members; the balance to be determined by the CVT Convenor according to the size and geographical distribution of the unit(s) to be visited. The CVT Convenor will appoint an experienced member to be the visiting team leader. The team leader will make the preliminary arrangements, co-ordinate and supervise the activities of the team members, chair the introductory and feedback meetings, and arrange for the timely submission of the final report and the associated documentation.

b Patients-Only Visits

A patients-only visit will be carried out by at least one Commission member and one or more visiting members, depending upon the size and geographical distribution of the unit(s) to be visited and the likely number of detained patients. The CVT Convenor will appoint an experienced member to be the visiting team leader. The team leader will make the preliminary arrangements, co-ordinate and supervise the activities of the team members, and arrange for the timely submission of the report and the associated documentation.

Wherever possible the team which is to visit a Regional/Medium Secure Unit should include a psychiatrist with forensic experience and, if the Convenor considers it necessary, arrangements can also be made for a member of a Special Hospital Panel, or a member with experience of Special Hospitals, to join the CVT visiting team. It may also be necessary to consider including a member with experience of adolescent patients and/or those with learning difficulties.

12 Meetings with SSD Representatives

Meetings with representatives of Social Services Departments should be held at least every two years and, whenever it is practical and acceptable to do so, should be arranged to coincide with full visits to hospitals and/or Registered Mental Nursing Homes. Separate meetings may be arranged on request or by mutual agreement. It is for the CVT Convenor to determine how many members of the Commission will be required if separate meetings are to be arranged.

It is important that at least one social work member of the Commission be included in the team which is to meet representatives of Social Services Departments. If no such member of the CVT is available, arrangements should be made for a social work member from another CVT to attend.

13 Conflicts of Interest

Subject to the specific guidance set out below, it is for each member of the Commission to decide whether his/her involvement in a particular Commission activity is likely to result in a conflict of interest that might be detrimental to the reputation of the Commission or to any of its functions. In cases of doubt advice should be sought from the CVT Convenor.

No member of the Commission should visit, investigate complaints, or perform any other Commission duties directly connected with any organisation or unit by which they are employed.

Where a member of the Commission has previously been employed by any of the organisations or units to be visited, it is for the member concerned to decide whether sufficient time has elapsed since the termination of that employment to enable him/her to visit without a conflict of interest arising.

No member of the Commission should investigate a complaint by, on behalf of, or about any person with whom he/she is, or has been involved in any capacity other than as a member of the Commission.

14   Visiting Team Tasks

The main tasks of the visiting team are outlined below; the visiting team leader should ensure that the tasks allocated to the individual members of the team are in conformity with the levels of responsibility indicated in the job descriptions.

So far as time constraints allow, the visiting team should aim to:-
i.   attend a short, initial meeting with representatives of the senior management group;
ii.   meet those detained patients who have asked to meet a member of the Commission and make personal contact with as many other detained patients as possible;
iii. visit the accommodation and facilities used by, or available to, the detained patients;
iv.   monitor the operation of the Act and the Code of Practice, examine the documents relating to the detention of patients, both past and present, and examine the policies and the procedural documents relating to the Act;
v.   meet with representatives of the main purchasers;
vi.   enquire into those issues identified by the Commission Management Board and/or the CVT Convenor as requiring particular attention;
vii. monitor the quality of care provided and other related issues
viii. attend the final feedback meeting; and
ix.   complete the relevant documentation and reports.

15   SSD Meetings - Team Tasks

So far as time constraints allow, team members should aim to:-
i.   attend an initial meeting with representatives of the senior management group;
ii.   meet with ASWs;
iii. meet with clients, including those subject to guardianship, who have requested an interview;
iv.   meet other groups of mental health workers (CPNs etc.), voluntary organisations and user groups;
v.   meet with representatives of other statutory groups, e.g. police, probation and ambulance services;
vi.   visit selected social services accommodation and facilities;
vii. monitor the use of the Mental Health Act and the Code of Practice, and examine the policies and procedural documents relating to the Act;
viii. enquire into those issues identified by the Commission Management Board as requiring particular attention;

ix. attend the final feedback meeting; and

x. complete the relevant documentation and reports.

16   Hours of Attendance

The normal expectation is that team members will, ordinarily, spend not less than six hours in the hospital/Registered Mental Nursing Home, or in meetings with representatives of Social Services Departments, on each of the scheduled duty days. Attendance during visits to hospitals/Registered Mental Nursing Homes need not be limited to normal office hours. It may sometimes be more effective to organise attendance on a sessional basis to enable some members of the team to visit during the evening or at night. Such visits can be helpful in enabling the visiting team to make a more rounded assessment of living conditions and the general standard of patient care. To this end, the organisation and timetabling of visits should provide an opportunity for some team members to attend outside normal office hours.

17   Meeting Patients/Clients

Meetings with individual patients/clients in private should normally be undertaken by a single member of the Commission, though it may sometimes be necessary or prudent for two persons to be present. It is for each visiting team to determine, after consulting the unit staff, whether the prevailing circumstances require that either a second member of the Commission and/or a member of staff should be in attendance when a patient/client is interviewed in private. Newly appointed members of the Commission should always be accompanied by an experienced member for the first few meetings with individual patients or clients.

If a member of the Commission receives a complaint from, or on behalf of, a patient/client and it cannot be resolved to the satisfaction of the complainant during the visit or shortly thereafter, the Commission's complaints procedure may have to be initiated (see separate complaints policy and procedure document). If the matter(s) raised by a patient can be dealt with during the course of the visit or the meeting, the visiting member should document the issues raised, the action taken and the outcome.

Before leaving the hospital arrangements will be made for each patient who has been interviewed by a member of the Commission, to receive a handwritten letter summarising the issues raised during their meeting, together with an outline of any further action which, with the agreement of the patient, is to be taken by the Commission. A record should also be kept of those patients not formally interviewed but with whom personal contact was made.

18   Programme of Visit and Meetings

Each CVT Convenor is responsible for devising an annual programme of CVT visits and meetings. The Convenors' group will discuss and, if necessary, revise the proposed annual programmes. The Chief Executive will arrange for these programmes, together with other bids for Commission activities, to be considered by the Commission Management Board.   Each CVT Convenor will then be allocated a budget against which the cost of the fees and allowances will be debited. It is the responsibility of the CVT Convenor to make such changes to the programme as are necessary to ensure that costs are contained within the budgetary allowance.

19   Responsibility for Organising Visits and Meetings

a   *The CVT support staff* are responsible for:-
  i.   making the preliminary arrangements;
  ii. providing the units to be visited, and/or the relevant Social Services Department, with at least three months notice of the dates of the visit and/or SSD meetings;
  iii. ensuring that the visiting team leader is given adequate and timely information, e.g. a copy of the previous report(s) and the response(s), and the name of the liaison person to enable personal contact to be established;
  iv. ensuring that the team members receive the appropriate information packs at least two weeks prior to the visit or SSD meeting;
  v.   arranging for the team's report to be despatched to the addressees, to the CVT Convenor and to the participating members not later than five weeks after the conclusion of the visit and/or the SSD meetings; and
  vi. arranging for the appropriate follow up action to be taken after the visit and/or SSD meetings.

b   *The leader of the Commission team* is responsible for:-
  i.   contacting the nominated liaison person in the Trust, Registered Mental Nursing Home and/or Social Services Department to finalise the programme and the timetable of visits and/or meetings with SSD representatives;
  ii. preparing a list of issues to be raised by the team at the initial meeting with senior managers;
  iii. allocating tasks to other members of the team and for co-ordinating their activities;
  iv. obtaining additional information about recent developments, current problems etc.;

v. chairing the initial and feedback meetings;

vi. ensuring that the relevant visit documentation and reports are completed; and

vii. drawing to the attention of the CVT Convenor and/or the Chief Executive, any matter arising from the visit and/or meetings with SSD representatives which gives cause for concern.

c. The *person responsible for writing the report* is responsible for arranging for the final draft report of the visit and/or SSD meetings to be sent to the CVT support staff not later than three weeks after the conclusion of the visit and/or SSD meetings;

d. *The CVT Convenor,* in consultation with the CVT Executive Officer, is responsible for monitoring the procedures and for reviewing the report(s), the associated documentation, and the response(s) to identify matters for attention on the next visit and/or SSD meeting, for discussion at CVT meetings or for referral elsewhere.

20 Liaison With Other Bodies

Each CVT will normally liaise directly with the Health Authorities, other purchasing bodies, NHS Trusts and any other hospitals and Registered Mental Nursing Homes authorised to hold detained patients within their visiting areas. Liaison with the Home Office, the Welsh Office, other government departments and with professional bodies, will normally be conducted through the Chief Executive.

21 Amendments to the Policy and Procedures

Suggestions for modifying the CVT visiting policy and/or the associated procedures should be submitted in writing to the Chief Executive through the CVT Convenor. The same procedure should be adopted if members of the Commission wish to make suggestions for amending the list of matters requiring particular attention.

8.2 Special Hospital Visiting Policy

PART A
The Policy for Visiting Special Hospitals

1 The Commission Remit

The Commission's visiting remit is defined in the Mental Health Act 1983 as follows:

"SECTION 120(1) - The Secretary of State shall keep under review the exercise of the powers and the discharge of the duties conferred or imposed by the Act so far as relating to the detention of patients or to patients liable to be detained under this Act and shall make arrangements for persons authorised by him in that behalf

a   To visit and interview in private patients detained under this Act in hospital and mental nursing homes;"

NB: The term "hospital" includes the three Special Hospitals.

2 Access to Records

DHSS Circular HC(83)19 directs authorities to make arrangements to ensure that:

"Any records which are required to be made under the Mental Health (Hospitals, Guardianship and Consent to Treatments) Regulations 1983 (SI 1983/893) and which relate to the detention or treatment of a patient of the hospital for which the authorities are responsible, are kept for a period of not less than five years commencing on the date on which the person to whom they relate ceases to be a patient in that hospital"

The circular also empowers any person "authorised by the Mental Health Act Commission for the purpose of carrying out any review mentioned in Section 120(1) of the Mental Health Act 1983 to:

"Require the production of and inspect any records relating to the detention or treatment of any person who is or has been detained in a hospital for which the authority is responsible."

3 Purpose of Visits

Visits by Commission members and visiting members to Special Hospitals have, broadly speaking, a fivefold purpose:

    a. to meet with detained patients, particularly those who have asked to see members of the Commission; meetings may be with individual patients or with groups of patients, including Patients' Councils;

b. to observe the conditions in which patients are detained;

c. to see how the provisions of the Mental Health Act 1983 and the Code of Practice are being applied;

d. to offer advice and guidance on the implementation of the Act; and

e. to review decisions to withhold a postal packet addressed to a patient;

Panel members are expected to behave in such a way as to ensure that:

a. the dignity of all patients is respected;

b. the patients' legitimate concerns are considered equitably and pursued with vigour;

c. issues of race, culture, gender and disability are fully acknowledged and respected;

d. all patients are kept fully informed of any action taken by the Commission on their behalf;

e. records of interviews, meetings and issues raised are accurately maintained and appropriate follow-up action taken without delay;

f. the operation of the Special Hospital Complaints' Procedure is routinely monitored;

g. there is effective interaction with patients, the groups representing patients (including the Patients' Council and Advocacy Service), the clinical staff and the Hospital Management Teams.

4 Frequency of Visits

The frequency of visits to Special Hospitals will be determined by the Panel Convenor, whose responsibility it is to ensure that at least once a year the statutory documents and treatment plans of each patient are reviewed, and that each patient is contacted and given the opportunity to meet with a member of the Commission in private.

There is no requirement for all visits to take place during normal office hours, indeed, it may sometimes be more appropriate to visit in the evenings, at night or at the weekend. Such visits should be helpful in enabling Panel members to make a more rounded assessment of living conditions and the general standard of patient care. To this end the Team Leaders should arrange for some visits to be undertaken outside normal office hours

5 Routine Visits

Most visits to Special Hospitals are organised on a clinical directorate/ward basis and take place during normal office hours, i.e. between 9.00 am and 5.00 pm, during which the team members will meet patients and hold discussions with the

Ward Managers and other members of the clinical teams. Members of the visiting teams will also pay periodic visits to specialist departments and off-ward areas as directed by the Panel Convenor or Team Leader.

6 Targeted Visits

From time to time the Commission will undertake extra visits as part of targeted exercises or thematic reviews, during which particular issues will be investigated, e.g. the use of seclusion facilities. These visits may be routinely notified, unannounced, short notice or out of hours visits.

7 Patients Only Visits

Convenors may arrange for some visits to be undertaken solely for the purpose of meeting detained patients. Such visits may be either instead of, or in addition to, a routine visit and may be out of hours, unannounced or short notice visits as circumstances require.

8 Unannounced Visits

It is neither necessary or nor desirable that prior notice should always be given of the Commission's intention to visit. It has been decided that at least 30% of all visits to Special Hospitals will be unannounced; these visits may be either routine, out of hours, patients-only or targeted visits. Convenors must notify the SHP Executive Officer in advance of any unannounced visit.

Because of the lack of notice it is likely that access to particular members of the hospital staff and to information, will be either limited or delayed. The visiting arrangements should be modified accordingly.

9 Short Notice Visits

Circumstances may arise in which it is considered that, although an unannounced visit would not be appropriate, the ward/unit should be given only very short notice of an intention to visit. In such cases, where the notice might be measured in hours rather than days, the limitations associated with Unannounced Visits may apply with almost equal force.

10 Out of Hours Visits

Arrangements should be made for Panel members periodically to visit patients and/or facilities in the evenings or at weekends. Such visits may be either Routine, patients-only or targeted visits, and may be either routinely notified, unannounced or short notice visits.

11   Composition of the Special Hospital Panels and Visiting Teams

To facilitate the visiting process a number of Commission members will be allocated to each of the Special Hospital Panels (SHPs). A Convenor will be appointed to manage the work of each Panel and will select those members of the Commission who are to be Team Leaders. The number of Team Leaders will be determined by the organisational structure of the hospital and will usually be related to the number of clinical directorates. It should be noted that throughout this document the term "clinical directorate" also applies to what is known at Broadmoor Special Hospital as a "Unit". Where the term "unit" is used in this document, it applies to a section of the hospital other than a ward or directorate and may, in some contexts, be synonymous with the term "department".

Each Team Leader will be responsible for a visiting team comprising both members and visiting members so as to provide a balance of skills, both personal and professional, taking into account the wards/units/directorates to be visited and the issues likely to arise. Gender and ethnic mix will also be taken into account.

The Team Leader will be responsible for the co-ordination of visits, and for maintaining communication with the Convenor, and others, on all matters related to their associated clinical directorate which fall within the Commission's remit.

Visits to a Special Hospital will always be led by a member of the Commission.

12   Panel Meetings

The SHP Convenor will arrange for all members of the Panel to meet together at least twice in each financial year.

13   The Core Team

The work of individual visiting teams is normally focused on issues arising within particular wards/directorates. In order to obtain a more comprehensive view of the whole hospital each SHP will establish a Core Team, to be composed of the Convenor and the Team Leaders, who will be responsible for examining hospital-wide issues. Other Panel members with specialist skills or experience may be invited to participate in particular Core Team projects.

14   Core Team Visits

The Core Team of each Panel will undertake a programme of special visits to examine particular aspects of the work of the hospital and the treatment of patients. The programme of work will be decided by the Convenor in consultation with the Team Leaders, and the outcome of their work will be reported to all Panel members either by correspondence or during meetings of the whole Panel. This programme will be in addition to the routine and other visits identified below, which will normally be undertaken by all members of the Panel.

15   Team Leaders

In addition to their role as members of the Core Team the Team Leaders, under the direction of the Convenor, will participate in:

    a. periodic meetings of Team Leaders;

    b. the planning of the annual programme of Panel activities;

    c. the monitoring of those policy issues which have been identified by the Commission Management Board as requiring particular attention;

    d. the monitoring of agreed quality standards;

    e. the review, in accordance with Section 121 of the Mental Health Act, of decisions to withhold postal packets;

    f. the identification of issues to be discussed at meetings with:

        i. the hospital senior management team;

        ii. SHSA / relevant purchasing authorities.

    g. meetings with the hospital senior management team at least twice yearly;

    h. the maintenance of effective communications with all Panel Members; and

    i. the formulation of issues to be considered for inclusion in the Biennial Report;

The Convenor will invite one of the Team Leaders to deputise as Convenor in his/her absence.

16   Conflicts of Interest

Subject to the specific guidance set out below, it is for each Panel member to decide whether his/her involvement in a particular activity is likely to result in a conflict of interest that might be detrimental to the reputation of the Commission or to any of its functions. In cases of doubt advice should be sought from the SHP Convenor.

Panel members should not visit, investigate grievances, or perform any Panel duties directly connected with any organisation or unit by which they are employed.

Where a Panel member has previously been employed by the hospital or any of the units to be visited, it is for the individual concerned to decide whether sufficient time has elapsed since the termination of that employment to enable him/her to visit without a conflict of interest arising.

No Panel member should investigate a grievance by, on behalf of, or about any person with whom he/she is, or has been, involved in any capacity other than as a Panel member.

17 Panel/Team Tasks

On routine visits, and so far as time constraints allow, Panel members should aim to:

a. attend a short, initial meeting with a staff member of the ward/unit to be visited;

b. meet those detained patients who have asked to meet a member of the Commission and make personal contact with as many other detained patients as possible;

c. visit the accommodation and facilities used by, or available to, the detained patients;

d. monitor the operation of the Act and the Code of Practice, examine the documents relating to the detention and treatment of patients, and examine the policies and the procedural documents relating to the Act and to the treatment of patients;

e. enquire into those issues identified by the Commission Management Board and/or the SHP Convenor as requiring particular attention;

f. monitor the quality of care provided and other related issues;

g. attend feedback meetings; and

h. complete the relevant documentation and reports. An Aide- Memoire and Check-List has been included and is available for use at the Convenor/Team Leaders' discretion. A supply of forms will be provided in the secure cabinet.

18 Hours of Attendance

The duration of visits will be determined by the Panel Convenor who will take account of such factors as the number of detained patients, the size, nature and geographical distribution of the wards and other units to be visited, and the experience of previous visits. The normal expectation is that Panel members will spend not less than six hours in the hospital on each visit.

19 Meeting Patients

Meetings with individual patients in private should normally be undertaken by a single Panel member; though it may sometimes be necessary or prudent for two persons to be present. It is for each Panel member to determine, after consulting the unit staff, whether the prevailing circumstances require that either a second Panel member and/or a member of staff should be in attendance when a patient is interviewed in private. Newly appointed members of the Panel and those under training, should always be accompanied by an experienced Panel member for the first few meetings with individual detained patients.

Panel members must compile a summary of the matters discussed during meetings with patients. Before leaving the hospital, arrangements will be made for each patient who has been interviewed by a member of the Commission to receive a handwritten letter which summarises the issues raised during their meeting, together with an outline of any further action which it was agreed would be taken by the Commission. There may be circumstances in which a patient would prefer that what transpired during the meeting was not recorded in this way, in which case a simple acknowledgement that a meeting took place is all that is required. Care should be taken to ensure that confidentiality is not compromised, and in that context the wishes of the patient should always be sought and respected.

An important element of the Commission's role with regard to grievances and complaints in Special Hospitals is to encourage the patients to make use of the Patients' Council, the local advocacy service (where it exists) and, for the more serious matters, the Special Hospital Complaints Procedure, which is routinely monitored by the Commission.

If a Panel member receives a complaint from, or on behalf of, a patient and it cannot be resolved to the satisfaction of the complainant during the visit or shortly thereafter, the patient should be advised to use those facilities. If any further action by the Commission becomes necessary it may fall within the terms of reference of the Commission Complaints Policy and Procedure.

If the matters raised by, or on behalf of, a patient can be dealt with during the visit, it may not be appropriate to advise the use of the formal complaints procedures, at least in the first instance. In such circumstances the Panel member should take particular care to summarise the discussion, document the action taken and the outcome on the Patient Meeting Record.

20   Visiting Programmes

Each Panel Convenor is responsible for devising an annual programme of Panel visits and meetings. The Convenors' group will discuss, and if necessary revise, the proposed annual programmes. The Chief Executive will arrange for these programmes, together with other bids for Commission activities, to be considered by the Commission Management Board. Each SHP Convenor will then be allocated a budget against which the cost of fees and allowances will be debited. It is the responsibility of the SHP Convenor to make such changes to the programme as are necessary to ensure that costs are contained within the budgetary allowance.

21 Responsibility for Organising Visits

a. *The SHP support staff* are responsible for:-

    i. establishing a secure filing system in each Special Hospital to hold copies of all relevant correspondence from the office files, stationary items including pads of VISIT 1 (S) and VISIT 2 (S), and copies of the Aide-Memoire and Check-List;

    ii. providing the Unit General Manager of each Special Hospital and the Secretary of the Patients' Council with the names of Panel members and, where appropriate, the composition of each team and the associated wards/units/directorates.

    iii. providing the Unit General Manager of each Special Hospital and the Secretary of the Patients' Council with an annual schedule of all routine visits to be undertaken. Confirmation of the scheduled visits will be sent to each clinical directorate on a quarterly basis;

    iv. sending a copy of all relevant correspondence to the hospital for the attention of the Team Leader on the next visit;

    v. informing the Team Leader of the names of those patients who have not had a private meeting with a member of the Commission in the preceding nine months;

    vi. drawing the attention of the Convenor to relevant correspondence received in the MHAC office;

    vii. arranging for the visiting team leader's report of the visit to be despatched to the hospital, as soon as possible and not later than three weeks after the conclusion of the visit; and

    viii. arranging for the appropriate follow up action to be taken after each visit.

b. *The Visiting Team Leader* is responsible for:-

    i. opening the mail addressed to the Team Leader and arranging for it to be filed in the secure cabinets;

    ii. obtaining additional information about recent developments, current problems etc.;

iii. preparing a list of issues to be raised by the team at the initial meeting with staff from the ward/unit to be visited;

iv. allocating tasks to other members of the visiting team and co-ordinating their activities;

v. chairing the initial and final meetings with ward/unit/staff;

vi. ensuring that all Patient Meeting Records and the associated Confirmatory Letters are completed and filed before the team leave the hospital;

vii. arranging for the top copy of each patient's Confirmatory Letter to be delivered;

viii. sending a copy of each Patient Meeting Record and the associated Confirmatory Letter to the MHAC office at the end of the visit;

ix. ensuring that a report of the visit, in the form of a letter to the ward manager, is drafted and sent to the SHP support staff not later than two weeks after the conclusion of the visit.

c. *Team Leaders* are responsible for:-

i. devising and implementing a detailed programme of work to be undertaken by the members of the visiting team;

ii. maintaining the hospital-based filing system for their allocated directorate/wards;

iii. dealing with team/directorate related correspondence;

iv. conducting discussions with senior members of the hospital staff;

v. reporting significant issues, concerns and events to the SHP Convenor;

vi. drafting periodic reports to the Clinical Directors; and

vii. monitoring the performance of Team members.

d. *The Convenor*, in consultation with the SHP Executive Officer, is responsible for:

i. reviewing the reports of visits and any responses;

ii. identifying matters to be raised on subsequent visits in consultation with Team Leaders;

iii. chairing Panel, Core Team and Team Leaders' meetings, together with such other meetings as are necessary for the effective conduct of the work of the Panel;

iv. directing and monitoring the performance of Panel members and the timeliness of visiting procedures;

v. arranging periodic meetings with the Patients' Council;

vi. compiling a biannual account of the Panel's activities for the Chairman of the Patients' Council; and

vii collating information and submitting a first draft of material for inclusion in the Biennial Report.

22   Liaison Arrangements

Meetings are held with representatives of the Special Hospitals Service Authority at least twice a year, at which the Commission is normally represented by the Chairman, the Chief Executive and the SHP Convenors. A copy of the minutes of each meeting is subsequently sent to all Panel members. Arrangements will be made for similar meetings to be held with representatives of the High Security Commissioning Board which is to succeed the SHSA after April 1996.

The three SHP Convenors meet regularly under the chairmanship of the Chief Executive. From time to time arrangements will be made for individual members to join a visit to another Special Hospital or to other secure facilities to broaden their experience.

Each SHP Convenor should arrange for one or two members of the Panel to attend a meeting of the Patients' Council (subject to their agreement) at least twice a year and, if possible, more frequently. The Convenor and the SHP Executive Officer should jointly prepare and send a written account of the Panel's activities to the Chairman of the Patients' Council at least twice a year.

23   Amendments to the Policy and Procedures

Suggestions for modifying the SHP visiting policy and/or the associated procedures should be submitted in writing to the Chief Executive through the SHP Convenor. The same procedure should be adopted if members of the Commission wish to make suggestions for amending the list of matters requiring particular attention.

8.3   Policy on Race and Culture

Introduction

British society is composed of people from various ethnic groups. Racial discrimination and insensitivity to cultural differences result in disadvantages being experienced by persons belonging to (or perceived as belonging to) these ethnic groups.

The Race Relations Act 1976 defines two kinds of racial discrimination:

• Direct discrimination arises where a person treats another person less favourably on racial grounds than he treats, or would treat, someone else. 'Racial grounds' means any of the following grounds: colour, race, nationality (including citizenship) or ethnic or national origins.

- Indirect discrimination consists of treatment which may be described as equal in a formal sense as between different racial groups but discriminatory in its effect on one particular group. A 'racial group' is one defined by reference to one or more of the following: colour, race, nationality (including citizenship) or ethnic or national origins.

Cultural differences between people or groups of people arise from differences in first language, norms with respect to behaviour and values, concepts of illness, attitudes towards the agencies that provide therapy and help for people in distress, etc.

The Mental Health Act Commission is committed to upholding Race Relations legislation and to being sensitive to the cultural needs of all sections of society through the following aims and actions.

1 Aims

1.1 To ensure equality of opportunity to all members of staff of the Commission to participate in the organisation and work the Commission irrespective of race, colour or nationality.

1.2 To ensure that detained patients and others dealt with by the Commission are treated equally, irrespective of race etc. (as above).

1.3 To ensure that any advice given by the Commission is free of racial discrimination and sensitive to cultural differences.

2 Action

2.1 Prevent and counteract the effects of discriminatory practice on racial grounds by any member of the Commission, its staff or anyone acting on behalf of the Commission.

2.2 Ensure that issues concerning racial and cultural matters are not 'marginalised'; such 'marginalisation' being construed as 'indirect discrimination' and treated as such under this policy.

2.3 Work towards establishing an ethnic mix of its membership and staff that reflects the ethnic composition of British society.

3 Recruitment and Membership

3.1 The Commission will seek to recruit members from all ethnic groups.

3.2 The Commission will keep under review the ethnic composition of its membership and seek to remedy any imbalance that may emerge.

3.3 The Commission will endeavour to ensure that all its members are involved in the work of the Commission according to their knowledge, experience and contracts of appointment, taking note of any special knowledge they may have through personal experience of racial and cultural issues; no member of the Commission or staff of the Commission will be excluded from any of the Commission's activities on the grounds of race.

4 Monitoring

4.1 The Commission will study and report on issues of race and culture as they relate to the Commission's work.

4.2 The Commission will promote a greater understanding within the Commission of matters relevant to race and culture.

4.3 The Commission will keep under review its policies, procedures and practices so that they reflect that understanding.

5 Training

5.1 The Commission will provide training to all members and staff of the Commission in order that in their work on behalf of the Commission they may:

5.2 Become aware of personal racism, racist practices and behaviour, and the ways in which racism may be counteracted within the Commission.

5.3 Become aware of racism and cultural differences in concepts of mental illness, diagnosis and behaviour.

5.4 Develop an understanding of the relevance to mental health and illness of cultural diversity in norms and attitudes.

5.5 Recognise racism within mental health services and develop ways of advising agencies on counteracting racism.

5.6 Recognise the cultural needs of detained patients and develop ways of advising agencies providing services for such patients so that their cultural needs are met.

6 Work of Commission

6.1 The Commission will ensure that its policies, procedures and activities are free of discriminatory practices on racial grounds.

6.2 The Commission will endeavour to ensure that Purchasers and Providers of mental health services for detained patients take adequate action to counteract racism within these services and to provide culturally sensitive services.

8.4   The Commission's Complaints Policy

1.   The Statutory Basis of the Commission's Complaints Remit

The statutory basis for the Commission's complaints remit is to be found at Section 120(1)(b) of the Act. There are two types of complaint that the Commission may investigate and guidance about them is set out in this handbook.

Section 120(2) gives to the Commission the discretion not to investigate a complaint or to discontinue a complaint where it is appropriate to do so.

2.   Objectives of Complaints Policy

The aim of the policy is to ensure that:

a)   Complaints received by the Commission are properly identified as falling within or without Section 120;

b)   Complaints are investigated promptly, effectively and fairly within a reasonable timescale;

c)   Where possible, conciliation between Complainant and the individual organisation complained about is undertaken and a settlement acceptable to the Complainant, and reasonable to the Commission, is achieved;

d)   The Complainant is kept fully informed of the progress of the complaints investigation;

e)   The result of the Commission's investigation and recommendations are reported to both the Complainant and those complained about;

f)   Where an investigation reveals that a detained person has not been cared for in accordance with the principles set out in the Code of Practice, or that the Mental Health Act has not been complied with, all appropriate steps are taken to remedy the situation and to ensure that what has happened does not recur; and

g)   The Commission monitors the exercise of its complaints remit and in particular the achievement of the objectives set out above.

3.   Terminology

A complaint for the purpose of this policy is any communication received by the Commission or any Commission members which:

a)   Falls within the Commission complaints remit as set out in Section 120(1)(b) of the Act; and

b)   In the case of such communications received by the Commission members while visiting hospitals or Registered Mental Nursing Homes that cannot be satisfactorily resolved during the visit and require action to be taken after the conclusion of the visit.

The definition includes complaints which merit investigation but cannot be investigated because the patient does not give or withdraws consent.

4. Time Limits

The following time limits should apply to Commission complaints investigations:

a) All complaints received in writing will be acknowledged in writing within two working days of receipt;

b) A more detailed response should be provided within three weeks of receipt of a Commission complaint. If this is not possible then an appropriate holding letter should be sent within that time;

c) The investigation of most Commission complaints should be concluded within fourteen weeks. Where circumstances prevent the achievement of this objective then the complainant should be informed and then kept further informed at not more than three weekly intervals; and

d) Where the investigation of a Commission complaint is not concluded within twenty weeks of receipt of the complaint, then the matter should be referred to the Chief Executive for review.

In order to ensure that the investigation of complaints is carried out as promptly as possible, the time limits referred to above should be adhered to in as many investigations as possible. It is important however, to ensure that compliance with the time limits is not to the detriment of the quality of the investigation. Where it is necessary to take longer than the time limits allow for, it is essential to keep the complainant informed.

8.5 Complaints Against Commissioners: Policy And Procedures

Policy and Procedure

This document sets out a policy and procedure for the Commission to follow when complaints against Commissioners are received from complainants apart from other Commissioners or Commission staff.

The Commission is a Health Authority and therefore the provisions of the Hospital Complaints Procedures Act 1985 apply.

1 The Policy

(a) Preface

All complaints to which this policy and procedures applies will be considered seriously and promptly and investigated thoroughly and fairly. All complaints are potentially valuable indicators of the Commission's performance and provide pointers by which the Commission's quality of service can be measured.

(b) Objectives

The objective of this policy is reconciliation on the basis of established facts. In the event that this is not possible, then the Vice-Chairman (in stage 1) or the Chairman (in stage II) will make a finding. (see below).

(c) Time Limits

Save in exceptional circumstances all complaints investigation under this policy should be completed within six weeks of receipt of the complaint.

2 Designated Officer

The Chief Executive is the Commission's "designated officer" to whom all complaints to which this policy refers will be referred. He will be responsible for ensuring that the Commission's policy and procedure is implemented in relation to each complaint received.

In stage 1 (see below) of the procedure the Vice-Chairman of the Commission will be informed of the progress of any complaints investigations and it will be the Vice-Chairman and not the designated officer who will make any provisional findings as to whether a complaint is justified. In stage II of the procedure it will be the Chairman who will (where necessary) make a finding as to whether a complaint is justified.

3 The Procedure

Stage I

(a) Receipt and initial action

All complaints received will be acknowledged by return and a copy of the complaints policy and procedure will be sent to the complainant. All complaints will be allocated a complaints against Commissioner number.

Where a complaint is received in writing, a copy of it will be sent immediately to the Commissioner's concerned for their comments.

Where a complaint is made verbally, a transcript of the complaint will be sent immediately to:

    i.   the complainant to check for accuracy;

    ii.   the Commissioner concerned for their comments.

Where necessary the designated officer (in consultation with the Vice-Chairman) will seek further information.

(b) Action after enquiries made

i. Complaints Report

Once the designated officer has received all the information referred to above, he will prepare a complaints report identifying any aspect of the complaint which are the subject of disagreement between the complainant and the Commissioner concerned. On completion, the designated officer will refer this to the Vice-Chairman.

ii. On receipt, the Vice-Chairman will decide if any further enquiries are necessary and if a meeting between the complainant and the Commissioners concerned is necessary to clarify any unresolved matters or to seek a resolution.

At this stage the Vice-Chairman will also offer a meeting to the Commissioner/s complained about.

iii. Once (ii) above is completed, then the Vice-Chairman will further consider the matter and make a decision as to:

a. whether the matter has been resolved and if so what action should be taken; or

b. in the absence of resolution whether the complaint is justified and what action should be taken. Such a finding will be a provisional finding.

Where the Vice-Chairman makes a provisional finding that the complaint is justified, then both the complainant and the Commissioner/s concerned will be notified immediately about the finding together with (in broad outline) the reasons supporting the finding. Both complainant and Commissioner will be advised that if they are dissatisfied with the finding, then they may request that the matter be referred to Stage II.

Stage II

(a) Where the complainant or Commissioner complained against disagrees with the provisional finding made by the Vice-Chairman, then they should notify the designated officer. On receipt of such notification the designated officer will refer the matter to the Chairman, who will:

i. where necessary call, on a designated officer to seek further information and/or

ii. recommend a further meeting between the complainant and the Commissioner concerned in order to clarify any misunderstandings, disputed facts or to seek a resolution of the matter.

(b) Where it is not possible to resolve the matter, the Chairman will then make a finding as to whether the complaint is justified and what action, if any, needs to be taken.

8.6   Complaints Against Soads: Interim Policy & Procedure

Policy and Procedure

This document sets out a policy and procedure for the Commission to follow when complaints against SOADs are received from complainants apart from other Commission members or Commission staff.

1   The Policy

Preface

> All complaints to which this Policy and Procedure applies will be considered seriously and promptly and investigated thoroughly and fairly. All complaints are potentially valuable indicators of the Commission's performance and provide pointers by which the Commission's quality of service can be measured.

Objectives

> The objective of this policy is reconciliation on the basis of established facts. In the event that this is not possible, then the NSC (Consent to Treatment) Convenor (in Stage I) or the Chairman of the Commission (in Stage II) will make a finding. (See below).

Time limits

> Save in exceptional circumstances all complaints investigation under this policy should be completed within six weeks of receipt of the complaint.

2   Designated Officer

The Complaints Coordinator is the Commission's 'designated officer' to whom all complaints to which this policy refers will be referred. He will be responsible for ensuring that the Commission's policy and procedure is implemented in relation to each complaint received. The Complaints Coordinator is authorised to delegate this duty as necessary.

In stage I (see below) of the procedure the NSC (Consent to Treatment) Convenor of the Commission will be informed of the progress of any complaints investigations and it will be the NSC (Consent to Treatment) Convenor and not the designated officer who will make any provisional finding as to whether a complaint is justified. In stage II of the procedure it will be the Chairman of the Commission who will (where necessary) make a finding as to whether a complaint is justified.

3   The Procedure

Stage 1

a) Receipt and initial action

All complaints received will be acknowledged by return and a copy of the complaints policy and procedure will be sent to the complainant. A complaints register will be maintained. All complaints will be allocated a registration number.

Where a complaint is received in writing, a copy of it will be sent immediately to the SOAD concerned for his or her comments.

Where a complaint is made verbally a transcript of the complaint will be sent immediately to:

   i. the complainant to check for accuracy;

   ii. the SOAD concerned for his or her comments.

Where necessary the designated officer (in consultation with the NSC (Consent to Treatment) Convenor, Policy EO and additional staff if appropriate will seek further information.

b) Action after enquiries made

   i.   Complaints report

   Once the designated officer has received all the information referred to above, he will prepare a complaints report identifying any aspects of the complaint which are the subject of disagreement between the complainant and the Second Opinion Appointed Doctor concerned. On completion the designated officer will refer this to the NSC (Consent to Treatment) Convenor.

   ii. On receipt the NSC (Consent to Treatment) Convenor will decide if any further enquiries are necessary and if a meeting between the complainant and the doctor concerned is necessary to clarify any unresolved matters or to seek a resolution.

   At this stage the NSC (Consent to Treatment) Convenor will also offer a meeting to the doctor complained about.

   iii. Once (ii) above is completed, then the NSC (Consent to Treatment) Convenor will further consider the matter and make a decision as to:

   a. whether the matter has been resolved and if so what action should be taken; or

   b. In the absence of resolution whether the complaint is justified and what action should be taken. Such a finding will be a provisional finding.

   Where the NSC (Consent to Treatment) Convenor makes a provisional finding that the complaint is justified, then both the complainant and the doctor/s concerned will be notified immediately about the finding together with (in broad outline) the reasons supporting the finding. Both complainant and doctor will be advised that if they are dissatisfied with the finding, then they may request that the matter be referred to Stage II.

Stage II

a) Where the complainant or SOAD complained against disagrees with the provisional finding made by the NSC (Consent to Treatment) Convenor then they should notify the designated officer. On receipt of such notification the designated officer will:

   i.   where necessary call on a designated officer to seek further information; and/or

   ii.   recommend a further meeting between the complainant and the doctors concerned. In order to clarify any misunderstandings, disputed facts or to seek a resolution of the matter.

b) Where it is not possible to resolve the matter, the Chairman of the Commission will then make a finding as to whether the complaint is justified and what action (if necessary) needs to be taken.

8.7 Witholding of Mail and Commission Review Powers: Policy and Procedure

A Introduction

The powers of hospital managers to examine and withhold postal packets, and their duties when they exercise those powers, are set out in Section 134 of the Mental Health Act 1983 and the Mental Health (Hospital, Guardianship and Consent to Treatment) Regulations (S.1 1983 No. 893). Where a packet or anything contained in it is withheld the duties include notifying within 7 days the patient and, if known, the person by whom the packet was sent, of a right of review of the decision by the Mental Health Act Commission.

By Section 121(7) and (8) of the Act and the regulations, the Commission is given complete discretion in the way it should conduct this review (which must be made to it within 6 months of the receipt of the notice) and it may direct that the packet be not withheld.

B Procedures for the Exercise of the Commission's Powers:

1. Relevant Special Hospital Panel (SHP) Executive Officer or Visiting Commissioner receive "appeal" from patient and/or sender of package. This need not necessarily be in writing.

2. A minimum of two, and not more than 3 Commissioners nominated by the SHP Convenor to review the decision.

3. Relevant Executive Officer notifies hospital of receipt of "appeal" and the arrangements made by Commissioner to hear it, and asks for their written explanation of the ground for withholding the package or item within the terms of Section 134(1) and (2), and the details of the procedure they have followed.

4. A visit should be arranged at which the following actions should be taken.
   (a) If patient is appellant, Commissioners interview as on complaints visits.
   (b) If sender is appellant, Commissioners decide whether to invite him to be present of if written submission will suffice.
   (c) Commissioners should examine hospital's procedural documents to satisfy themselves that the requirements of the Act have been followed.
   (d) Commissioners to examine documents, articles etc., withheld.
   (e) Commissioners, at their discretion, to interview all staff who had any direct influence on the particular decision to withhold.
   (f) Commissioners to interview the person appointed by the Managers, who has withheld the package or item, especially if considering overriding the decision.

(NB: If appropriate and parties agree, Commissioners could interview appellant and parties (e) and (f) together)

5. Commissioners make decision and notify appellant(s) and Managers in writing. If the Commissioners think it is desirable, and especially if the patient is mentally impaired, they may also tell the patients verbally.

6. Commissioners consider whether cases raise any issues which should be reported to SHP team meeting, relevant National Standing Committee meeting or Central Policy Committee.

9 Mental Health Act Commission Statistics (Number of Visits/Complaints)

Number of visits undertaken to Mental Health Units and meetings with Social Services Departments:
July 1st 1993 to June 30th 1995

Table 6

Type of Hospital	Announced visits	Unannounced visits	Out of hours visits	Total number of visits	% of total Commission visits
hospital	814	41	24	879	65%
special hospital	231	4	0	236	17%
registered mental nursing home	53	3	0	56	4%
social services department	189	–	–	189	14%

Analysis of Issues Arising on Hospital Visits, extracted from Hospital Reports issued by the Commission

Complaints

KEY

1) Lack of independence in complaint procedure
2) Quality of investigation is variable
3) Not made clear to detained patients that they may appeal to the MHAC
4) Allegations of sexual assault not always pursued as a matter of course
5) Incomplete investigation of complaints

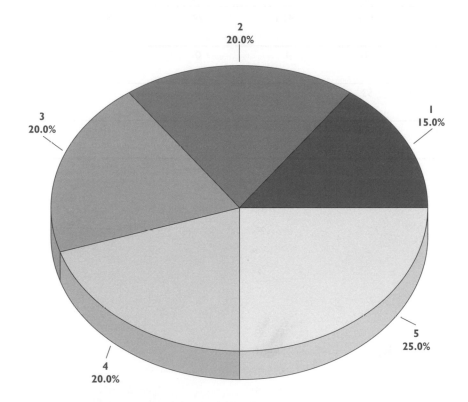

2
20.0%

3
20.0%

1
15.0%

5
25.0%

4
20.0%

KEY

1)   Drugs given don't match Form 38
2)   Inaccurate Form 38's
3)   Confusion amongst staff about purpose of Form 38
4)   No upper-dose limit included by RMO
5)   Form 38/39 not up to date
6)   RMO confuses consent form with other care plans
7)   Form 38 illegible
8)   Medication administered without check of consent Form 38
9)   Patients not told about nature/likely effect of drug
10)   Form 38 does not use BNF categories
11)   Form 38/39 not attached to the prescription card
12)   RMO did not seek valid consent prior to administration of drug
13)   Section 3 detained patients' consent is sometimes not sought
14)   Form 38's are completed outside the 3 month period
15)   Non-specified courses of ECT
16)   Status of Clozapine is not specified
17)   New form 38/39 not completed if medication is altered
18)   Consent status not checked when RMO takes over another consultants patient –
19)   Staff training in consent matters is needed
20)   Unauthorised alteration of a statutory form

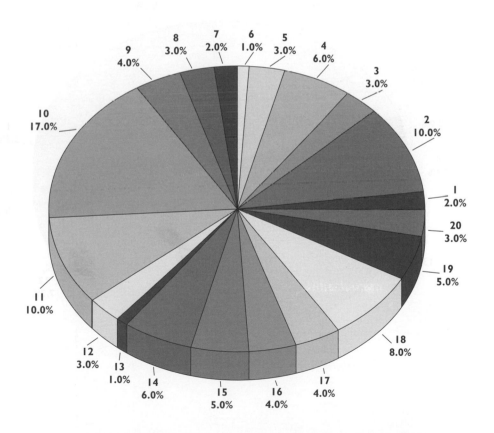

Section 17 Leave

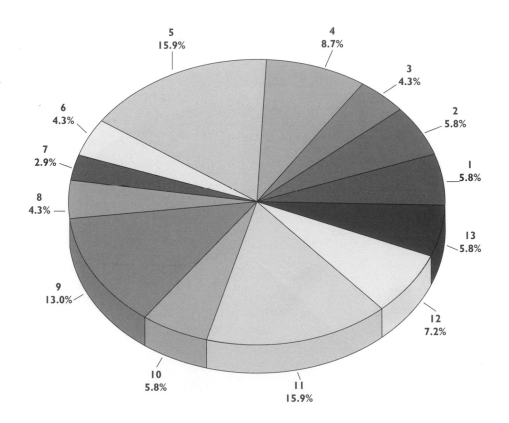

Section 117 Aftercare

KEY

1) **No case conference**
2) **Not enough planning for Aftercare**
3) **Patient not involved in plan**
4) **No specific allocation of keyworker**
5) **Limited aftercare facilities**
6) **Register needs updating**
7) **No uniform recording of Section 117**
8) **Staff show confusion over correct procedures**
9) **Difficulties in monitoring progress of patients**
10) **Relative & carers not involved**
11) **Policy of Aftercare – commended by Commission members**
12) **Policy of Aftercare – poor or not available**

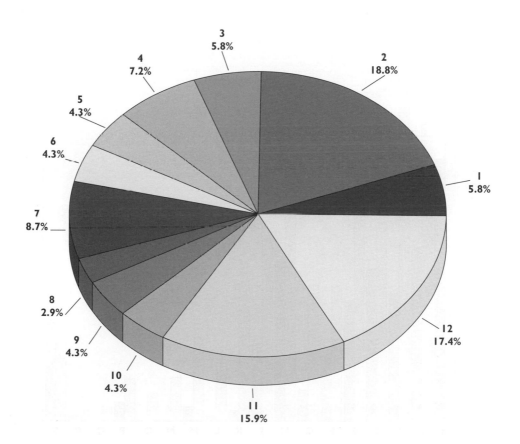

Total Number of Complaints received in each Category
1991-1993/1993-1995 (1 July-30 June)

COMPLAINTS CATEGORY CODES

A: Offences against the person
B: Medical care and services
C: Medical treatment
D: Nursing care and services
E: Other professional care and services
F: Domestic care, living arrangements, privacy
G: Finance, benefits, property
H: Deprivation of liberty
J: Leave, parole, transfer and other absences from hospital

K: Mental Health Review Tribunal matters
L: Family matters
M: Administration
N: Local Authority services/functions
O: Social educational, recreational matters
P: Ethnic, cultural, religious matters
Q: Department of Health, Home Office, other Government Departments
R: Mental Health Act Commission
S: Others

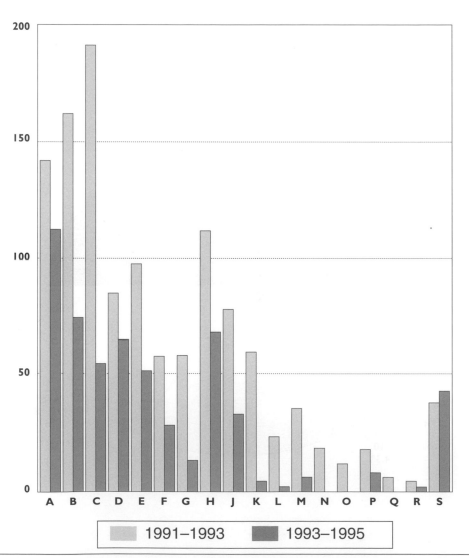

The Mental Health Act Commission: Sixth Biennial Report 1993–1995

Per cent of Complaints received in each Category
1991-1993/1993-1995 (1 July-30 June)

COMPLAINTS CATEGORY CODES

A: Offences against the person
B: Medical care and services
C: Medical treatment
D: Nursing care and services
E: Other professional care and services
F: Domestic care, living arrangements, privacy
G: Finance, benefits, property
H: Deprivation of liberty
J: Leave, parole, transfer and other
   absences from hospital

K: Mental Health Review Tribunal matters
L: Family matters
M: Administration
N: Local Authority services/functions
O: Social educational, recreational matters
P: Ethnic, cultural, religious matters
Q: Department of Health, Home Office, other
   Government matters
R: Mental Health Act Commission
S: Others

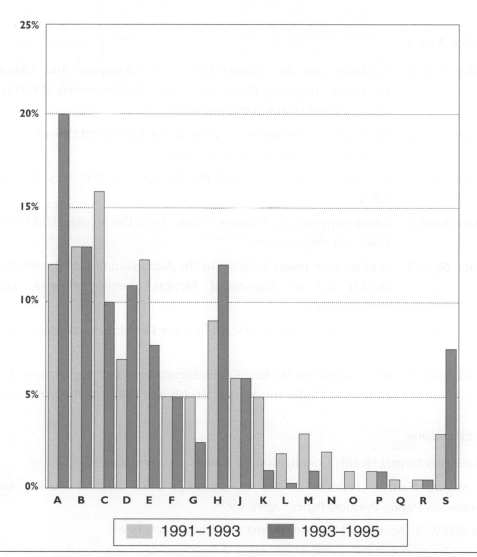

Information Leaflets for Patients, Relatives and Staff

General Information Leaflet

The Administration of Medication to Patients Detained Under the Mental Health Act

Practice Notes

Practice Note 1   Guidance on the Administration of Clozapine and Other Treatments requiring Blood Tests under the Provisions of Part IV of the Mental Health Act *June 1993*

Practice Note 2   Nurses, the Administration of Medicine for Mental Disorder and the Mental Health Act. *March 1994*

Practice Note 3   Section 5(2) of the Mental Health Act and Transfers. *March 1994*

Practice Note 4   Issues Surrounding Sections 17 and 18 of the Mental Health Act 1983. *(In Preparation)*

Practice Note 5   Guidance on Issues Relating to the Administration of the Mental Health Act in Registered Mental Nursing Homes. *(In Preparation)*.

Practice Note 6   A Guide to the Mental Health Act for General Practitioners. *(In Preparation)*.

Practice Note 7   Irregularities in Medical Recommendations and Applications for Detention Under the Mental Health Act 1983 *(In Preparation)*.

Miscellaneous

Guidance to Mental Health Commissioning Bodies   (In Preparation)

The Mental Health (Patients in the Community) Bill - Mental Health Act Commission Public Position Paper. April 1995

Form MHAC 1 (Section 61 Review Form) Revised March 1994

11 *Glossary*

ASW - APPROVED SOCIAL WORKER- A social worker approved under Section 114 of the Act to carry out assessments and other duties under the Act (see Code of Practice chapter 2, chapter 6.6)

BNF - BRITISH NATIONAL FORMULARY- A biannual publication by the British Medical Association and the Royal Pharmaceutical Society of Great Britain, the BNF is a list of all drugs and preparations, including recommended dose ceilings (BNF limits).

CODE OF PRACTICE - The 1983 Act requires that a regularly revised Code of Practice is published for the guidelines of those concerned in the admission and treatment of the mentally ill. The latest edition was published by HMSO in August 1993.

CPC - CENTRAL POLICY COMMITTEE- The Commission Central Policy Committee has overall responsibility for the activities of the Commission. Its functions will be partially replaced by a Management Board from 1st November 1995

CPN - COMMUNITY PSYCHIATRIC NURSE

CRE - COMMISSION FOR RACIAL EQUALITY

CVT - COMMISSIONER VISITING TEAM - Commission Members are assigned to one of seven visiting teams that cover different geographical areas of the country.

DHA - DISTRICT HEALTH AUTHORITIES

EMI - ELDERLY MENTALLY ILL

EO - EXECUTIVE OFFICER

FORM 39 - A form authorised by a SOAD indicating that, although the patient is unable, or refuses, to give consent to treatment, that treatment is necessary and should be given.

GMC - GENERAL MEDICAL COUNCIL

HMT - HOSPITAL MANAGEMENT TEAM

ISU - INTERIM SECURE UNIT

KEY WORKER - An identified person who has a defined responsibility towards a specific user of services, usually with some responsibility for service provision and the monitoring of care.

MHAC - MENTAL HEALTH ACT COMMISSION

NSC - NATIONAL STANDING COMMITTEE

OT - OCCUPATIONAL THERAPIST

PDU - PERSONALITY DISORDER UNIT

PLACE OF SAFETY - Under Section 136 the police may remove a person from a public place and take that person to a place of safety if they consider that that person is suffering from a mental disorder and is in immediate need of care and control. The place of safety is defines in the Act as any police station, prison or remand centre, or any hospital at the discretion of the managers.

RCP - ROYAL COLLEGE OF PSYCHIATRISTS

RMO - RESPONSIBLE MEDICAL OFFICER - Usually the consultant psychiatrist on the staff of the hospital to which a patient has been admitted; defined under Section 34 of the Act (see Jones [1994] 1-209).

RMP - REGISTERED MEDICAL PRACTITIONER

RSU - REGIONAL SECURE UNIT

SECLUSION - The supervised confinement of a patient alone in a room, which is locked for the protection of the patient or others from serious harm. (see Code of Practice 18.5-18.23)

SECTION 12 APPROVED DOCTOR - A Doctor approved by the Secretary of State to provide medical recommendations in applications to detain patients under the Act. Two medical recommendations are required, one of which must be from a Section 12 approved doctor. (see Jones [1994] 1-081)

SOAD - SECOND OPINION APPOINTED DOCTOR - A doctor appointed by the Secretary of State to give a second opinion treatment plans, and to authorise treatment given without consent under part iv of the Act.

SHP - SPECIAL HOSPITAL PANEL - Commission Members who visit one of the three Special Hospitals are members of the appropriate Special Hospital Panel. The SHP's are. from November 1st 1995, equivalent to CVT's in the structure of the Commission.

SHSA - SPECIAL HOSPITAL SERVICE AUTHORITY

SSD - SOCIAL SERVICES DEPARTMENT

Evaluation Sheet

Readers' Survey

The Mental Health Act Commission hopes that you have found this report useful and informative. We welcome your comments and suggestions for change in the future.

It would be helpful if readers would complete the questionnaire below by ticking the box of your choice and return it to the Commission.

Thank you for your assistance.

Please tick your Choice	1 Excellent	2 Very Good	3 Average	4 Good	5 Below Average	6 Poor
Content of Report						
Style						
Layout						
Statistical Information						
Presentation						

Please Include Your Comments Below:

(If you have ticked boxes 4 - 6 above, please indicate how you think the report could be improved).

Please return to: Mental Health Act Commission
Maid Marian House
56 Hounds Gate
Nottingham NG1 6BG

13 References

1. Reed, J (1994) Report of the Department of Health & Home Office Working Group on Psychopathic Disorder. DOH/Home Office, London.

2. Jones R (1994). "Mental Health Manual", 4th Edn, Sweet & Maxwell, pp 1-339

3. Law Commission Report (1995). "Mental Incapacity"; Law Commission Paper 231, HMSO

4. Review Article (1995). Law Commission on Mental Incapacity. Bulletin of Medical Ethics March, 13-18

5. Department of Health and Welsh Office (1983). "Code of Practice: Mental Health Act 1983". HMSO: London.

6. Department of Health Circulars (1989) "The discharge of patients from hospital". HC(89)5; "The care programme approach for people with a mental illness referred to the specialist psychiatric services" HC(90)23; "Guidance on the discharge of mentally disordered people and their continuing care in the community" HSG(94)27.

7. Curran, C and Zigmond, A (1994) The Use of Section 5(2). Psychiatric Care, May/June, 78-82

8. Gostin, L (1986), "Mental Health Services: Law and Practice", Shaw and Sons, London

9. Royal College of Psychiatrists (1993) "Consensus Report on the Use of High Dose Antipsychotic Medication", Council Report CR26

10. Banerjee, S, Bingley, W & Murphy, E (1995) Deaths of Detained Patients: a Review of Reports to the Mental Health Act Commission, Mental Health Foundation (In Press)

11. Joseph, P and Potter, M (1993) Diversion From Custody. I: Psychiatric Assessment at the Magistrate's Court. British Journal of Psychiatry, 162, 325-334

12. Hedderman, C. (1993) "Panel Assessment Schemes for Mentally Disordered Offenders", Home Office Research and Planning Unit, Paper 76.

13. Amendment to Social Security Regulations (1992) Mentally Disordered Persons Detained in Legal Custody Adjudication Officers Guide **Vol 2**, Part 17, 17036-17039.

14. NHS Executive (1995) Mental Health Task Force London Project: follow-up report. Department of Health

15. Calloway P, McKenna P, Tandon S (1994) Community Psychiatric Services. The Lancet, **344**,63

16. Forster R, Kandolf S, Laburda E, Mixa E (1994) Entwicklung und status quo der allgemein-psychiatrischen Versorgungsangebote in Ostereich. Gemeindenahe Psychiatrie, **49**,5-17

17. Mental Health Task Force (1994) Mental Health in London: Priorities for Action. Department of Health publication, 7

18. Government Statistical Department (1995) In-patients Formally Detained in Hospitals under the Mental Health Act (1983) and Other Legislation, England:1987-88 to 1992-93. Statistical Bulletin (Department of Health), **4**, March,1-26

19. Hollander D & Slater MS (1994) 'Sorry, no beds': a Problem for Acute Psychiatric Admissions. Psychiatric Bulletin, **18**, 532-534

20. Blom-Cooper L, Hally, H & Murphy, E (1994). "The Falling Shadow: One Patient's Mental Health Care" 1978-1993. Duckworth, London

21. Liebling H and McKeown (1995) Staff Perceptions of Illicit Drug Use Within a Special Hospital. Criminal Behaviour, Attributions and Rationality; British Psychological Society Issues in Criminological and Legal Psychology, **22**, 37-44

22. Zigmond A (1995).Special Care Wards: are they special? Psychiatric Bulletin, **19**, 310-312

14 Index

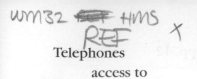

Printed in the United Kingdom for HMSO
Dd 301497, C32, 11/95, 39462, 336593